Political Traditions in Foreign Policy Series
Kenneth W. Thompson, Editor

CRACKING THE MONOLITH

CRACKING THE MONOLITH

U.S. Policy Against
the Sino-Soviet
Alliance, 1949–1955

DAVID ALLAN MAYERS

LOUISIANA STATE
UNIVERSITY PRESS
Baton Rouge and London

Designer: Diane B. Didier
Typeface: Linotron Times Roman
Typesetter: Moran Colorgraphic
Printer: Thomson-Shore, Inc.
Binder: John Dekker & Sons, Inc.

Some of the material that appears in Chapters IV and V was originally published in David Mayers, "Eisenhower's Containment Policy and the Major Communist Powers, 1953–1956," *International History Review*, V (February, 1983), 59–83. The author gratefully acknowledges the publisher's permission to use this material.

LIBRARY OF CONGRESS CATALOGING-IN-PUBLICATION DATA

Mayers, David Allan, 1951–
   Cracking the monolith.
   Bibliography: p.
   Includes index.
   1. United States—Foreign relations—China.
2. China—Foreign relations—United States.
3. United States—Foreign relations—Soviet Union.
4. Soviet Union—Foreign relations—United States.
5. Soviet Union—Foreign relations—China. 6. China—
Foreign relations—Soviet Union. 7. United States—
Foreign relations—1945–1953. 8. United States—Foreign
relations—1953–1961. 9. Korean War, 1950–1953—
Diplomatic history. I. Title.
E183.8.C5M382   1986   327.73051   86–40
ISBN 0-8071-1287-9

Publication of this book has been assisted by a grant from the Andrew W. Mellon Foundation.

For Odette, Eugene, Sara, and John

For thousands of years this most populous nation on earth has lived a concept of humanity as sublime as the West's though different from it. Her successfully claimed independence can be compared only superficially to Tito's, whose claim is bound to fail in the long run. If China, because of a world-political situation which America wanted, is a Russian ally for the time being, she is by no means a Russian satellite.

Though no longer a practical issue, it is not without historical interest to ask whether American policy might possibly have backed the Chinese Communists. Could America, by supporting China's totalitarian technological development, have won a great ally in world politics? What Russia has done could perhaps have been done more extensively and better by America: to send no soldiers but many technicians, to claim no advantages to China's detriment, to foster technological progress by extending massive credit. Was it dogmatic political prejudice that stood in the way? Or would China not have trusted the Americans in any case?

—Karl Jaspers, *The Future of Mankind*, 1958

CONTENTS

ACKNOWLEDGMENTS

This study is a result of conversations with the late Sir Alastair Buchan. He encouraged my research and was very stimulating and helpful. At later, critical junctures, my work was supported by the guidance, insight, and aid of Jeremy Azrael, John Gaddis, Akira Iriye, Morton Kaplan, and Tang Tsou.

I am indebted to the invaluable assistance of the staffs of the National Archives, Carrollton Press, Mudd Library at Princeton University, and Eisenhower and Truman libraries. Research funds were made available to me from the University of California at Santa Cruz.

Friends have also been generous with their reflections and experiences. Jeffery Levi shared his work and ideas about the issue of perception in international relations. Michael Smith helped me to define problems and refine ideas. The late George Lanyi, my mentor at Oberlin College, supplied the crucial moral support that only a wise and older friend can provide. At Santa Cruz, both students and colleagues have been kind and ready with helpful advice. Special thanks go to Isebill Gruhn, Peter Kenez, Bruce Larkin, Wendy Mink, and Bill Tetreault.

Finally, my wife, Elizabeth, has acted as chief critic, editor, and coach. She has been of immense help; without her the book would never have been written.

CRACKING THE MONOLITH

INTRODUCTION

The political unity that once characterized the communist world is today shattered beyond repair. Although the Soviet Union, the so-called Fatherland of Socialism, remains the single most powerful communist state, its leaders are no longer regarded as the ultimate authorities, either intellectually or politically, of world communism.

In 1948, Yugoslavia, under Marshal Tito, became the first Marxist country to break with the Soviet Union. Since then and despite periods of limited Soviet-Yugoslav detente, Belgrade has remained a rival to Moscow and has embodied an alternative political and ideological conception of communist organization. In more recent years in Eastern Europe, Romania and even little Albania have steered courses in foreign policy quite independent from the Soviet Union. Hungary enjoys a degree of liberalism in cultural and intellectual affairs that far surpasses that of any other member of the Warsaw Pact. The nonruling communist parties of Europe, principally the Italian and Spanish, have also demonstrated initiative independent of their past master, the Communist party of the Soviet Union (CPSU).

In the Far East, the fragmentation of world communism has been even more dramatic. Two decades ago, the People's Republic of China (PRC) defected from the Soviet fold and since then has promoted its own distinctive form of Marxist politics and economic development. The world has also witnessed military clashes along the Sino-Soviet frontier. In Southeast Asia, communist states have waged wars against each other. Though limited, the Chinese-Vietnamese war was fought in deadly earnest. The Vietnamese-Cambodian war has been a full-scale conflict and has provided grim but eloquent refutation of the national transcending qualities ascribed to communism by earlier theorists and idealists. It must have been with heartfelt conviction that Hu Yaobang, the Chinese Communist party leader, pronounced on the one hundredth anniversary of Marx's death in 1983 that the movement he inspired "has followed a tortuous course of development. It has scored magnificent successes and victories, but has also experienced severe setbacks and failures, undergoing a bewildering process of turbulence and division." [1]

The divisions within the communist world have enabled non-Marxist states to gain some advantage. In the early 1970s, Richard Nixon and Henry Kissinger pursued a flexible policy in which they tried to play China and the Soviet Union against each other so as to obtain leverage against each and against Hanoi. In recent years, the United States and China have cooperated to a modest degree in checking Soviet influence in the Far East. This cooperation has not led to a Sino-American alliance, tacit or otherwise, and indeed cooperation between the two countries has been fitful and immensely complicated by the problem of Taiwan. It is clearly in the interests of both countries, however, to prevent Soviet hegemony in the Far East, and this fact alone should be decisive in determining the future course of Sino-American relations.

If balance-of-power politics involving the United States with China and Russia in a great game of tripolar diplomacy is in the American interest, would the United States have benefited even earlier by establishing working relations with China during the 1960s or 1950s? Perhaps American recognition of Communist China in late 1949 would have helped avert Sino-American fighting in Korea and spared the United States from intervening in Vietnam against alleged Chinese proxy aggression. Perhaps, as Karl Jaspers suggested in 1958, the United States could even have won a great ally in world politics. Why did the United States fail to follow this reasonable course of action? We now know that intracommunist state relations in the late 1940s and early 1950s were hardly perfect. Just what was the official American perception of international communism during the most stormy period of the Cold War? Did American policy makers not discern any Sino-Soviet tensions, potential and actual, in the early 1950s? Was anything at all done to exploit difficulties between China and Russia to American advantage?

Standard interpretations suggest not. One line of analysis assumes that the

1. "Highlights of Hu Yaobang's Report," *Beijing Review*, XXVI (March 21, 1983), 5. For the sake of consistency with U.S. government documents from the 1950s, I will with few exceptions rely on the pre-1978 Romanization of Chinese names.

Americans were unaware of Sino-Soviet problems and, therefore, did not manipulate them. Harold Hinton claims in *The Bear at the Gate* that not until the late 1950s was it evident to sophisticated analysts, and not even then to policy makers, that serious problems plagued the Sino-Soviet alliance. He concludes, "Obviously a dispute whose existence was not recognized at the highest level in the United States could not be consciously exploited, regardless of whether objective opportunities to do so existed." Whereas Hinton merely asserts official American misperception about the true nature of the Sino-Soviet alliance, Adam Ulam goes further and ascribes blame. He faults Dwight D. Eisenhower and John Foster Dulles in particular for being insensitive to the contraditions underlying supposed communist solidarity. According to Ulam, American policy was burdened by blindness and failure as late as 1959. He also criticizes the Eisenhower administration for being both hopelessly complacent in its lackadaisical foreign policy and unwilling to improvise. Until 1960, Ulam laments, "protestations of the 'unshakeable friendship' between the USSR and the People's Republic were being taken in the West at face value." American policy amounted merely to a number of *ad hoc* responses to Chinese and Soviet initiatives, but containment never included so imaginative a policy as spoiling the opposition's alliance system. Probably American policy makers later welcomed Sino-Soviet problems that stemmed from mismanaged, clumsy efforts to coordinate strategy against the "imperialist threat." Such communist difficulties, Hinton and Ulam insist, were fortuitous rather than the result of deliberate American designs.[2]

Other authors, such as Lewis Purifoy and Richard Freeland, do not believe that American diplomacy was unduly burdened by a lack of perspicacity. Instead, they hold that American policy makers were not in any position to exacerbate or exploit Sino-Soviet problems; domestic constraints related to the McCarthy hysteria thwarted execution of any flexible policy, let alone one based on national differences between Russia and China. Purifoy argues that the Truman administration was forced by pressures from a hysterical, anticommunist domestic campaign to dispense with both rational thinking and moderate policy; but for McCarthyism, America probably would have avoided commitments to Chiang Kai-shek, granted recognition to China, allowed her admission to the United Nations, and been spared war in Korea and disaster in Southeast Asia. In Purifoy's view, Harry Truman and Dean Acheson unfortunately forsook sensible policies to protect themselves from the abuse of

2. Harold Hinton, *The Bear at the Gate* (Stanford, 1971), 85; Adam Ulam, *A History of Soviet Russia* (New York, 1976), 239.

Senator Joseph McCarthy and his ilk and pursued unworthy objectives designed solely to deflect criticism and domestic opponents. American politics led inexorably to an anticommunist foreign policy, labeled by Purifoy as "external McCarthyism." Related to the domestic variety by simple-mindedness and impassioned rhetoric, "external McCarthyism" trapped Truman into adopting a rigid, misconceived policy toward China. American diplomacy, according to Purifoy, was at the mercy of a demagogue. Policy makers had little choice but to suit diplomacy to rhetoric, which, employing such phrases as "monolithic communist threat" and "international conspiracy," did not allow for mutual suspicions between China and Russia or even their disagreement. Whatever diplomatic possibilities occurred were neglected, lost by timorous leaders in Washington. Freeland concurs with Purifoy's analysis and writes, "In the short period between the Truman Doctrine speech and early 1951 . . . the Administration had been led, against its will and policy, but according to the logic of its rhetoric and politics, to a full application of the Truman Doctrine in Asia." Forced to the defensive, the administration adopted a China policy that responded to political symbols rather than international realities.[3]

Within the past several years, a number of scholars have argued, based on previously classified papers, that several ranking American government officials knew about Sino-Soviet tensions before the Korean War but were ineffective in spoiling the alliance. John Gaddis contends that if the plans of Truman, George C. Marshall, and Acheson had succeeded, a multipolar international system—similar to the one later sought by Nixon and Kissinger—might have developed in the early 1950s. Yet once Sino-American fighting erupted in Korea, the idea of splitting the communist alliance was dropped; presumably, the areas of common concern between Moscow and Peking created a marriage resilient enough to withstand any American machinations. Gaddis maintains that the Americans were aware of this and therefore did not extend themselves much. Attempts at damaging the alliance played a minor role in Washington's policy, hardly providing a leitmotiv to the 1949–1955 period. In his words: "As a result [of the Korean War], men who had set out to exploit a Sino-Soviet split wound up instead encouraging Sino-Soviet unity. Rarely in recent history have short term considerations exerted such domi-

---

3. Lewis Purifoy, *Harry Truman's China Policy* (New York, 1976), xv; Richard Freeland, *The Truman Doctrine and the Origins of McCarthyism* (New York, 1974), 358.

nance over more distant ones; rarely have preoccupations of the present so tyrannized the future."[4]

Although all of the preceding explanations are helpful, they are ultimately insufficient. As will become clear, Washington policy makers between 1949 and 1955 were—to varying degrees—alert to tensions between the communist mainland allies. Not only were American officials aware of Soviet and Chinese suspicions of one another before Sino-American conflict in Korea, but the administration pursued a subtle plan, albeit finally ineffective, aimed at drawing China away from Soviet influence. Had this plan worked, China might then have played an independent role in diplomacy and contributed to a stable balance of power in the Far East.

American internal constraints in the early 1950s, reflecting and affecting world events, made prosecution of a pragmatic policy toward the Sino-Soviet alliance very difficult. Exaggerated policy rhetoric, partisan opposition, interest groups, and the China bloc in Congress undoubtedly hampered policy makers trying to advance American interests according to a realistic assessment of international power arrangements.[5] Yet contrary to the "diplomacy of hysteria" interpretation, McCarthy, his colleagues, and others, though bothersome and even dangerous, did not simply panic the administration, forcing it to adopt plans otherwise unimaginable. The truth, instead, rests somewhere between Purifoy's remark that Truman's foreign policy was "never

4. John Gaddis, "Was the Truman Doctrine a Real Turning Point?" *Foreign Affairs*, LII (January, 1974), 393.

5. The China bloc, composed of senators and representatives who supported the Nationalist cause and stressed an active Asian diplomacy over interests in Europe, stridently denounced the administration's China policy of the 1940s. Anticommunist and anti-Truman, the Republican and southern Democratic congressmen heaped abuse on Acheson for his "do-nothing" policy.

The bloc received support from Henry Luce, whose magazines, *Time* and *Life*, gave unqualified endorsement of Chiang's regime. Moral backing was also obtained from General Douglas MacArthur, "first of the Asia firsters." But in the "China Lobby," the bloc had its most natural ally and important champion. Funded by the Nationalist embassy in Washington, the "lobby" employed anticommunist businessmen and former military officers as propaganda agents. Chiang's brothers-in-law, H. H. Kung and T. V. Soong, vigorously campaigned to influence American policy favorably toward the Nationalists. Apparently, Soong once bragged to a State Department official, "There is practically nothing that goes on in your government of which I do not learn within three days."

Throughout the 1950s, the lobby sought to obtain economic and military support for Chiang, prevent American recognition of Peking, and ensure American opposition to a UN seat for Communist China. Over the years the lobby assumed different names, but its core membership remained constant. In 1953, the front organization's name was changed from Committee of One Million Against Admission of Communist China to the United Nations to the less cumbersome Committee of One Million, to which several dozen congressmen belonged.

intended to contain anything but the fury of the McCarthyites'' and Acheson's boast: ''A good deal of nonsense has been written about the effect of the attack of the primitives, before and during McCarthy's reign, on the China policy of the Truman administration. Whatever effect it had on our successors, it had little on us.''[6]

Post–Korean War Chinese hostility and fear of the United States, combined with popular anti-Chinese communist sentiments and lobby groups in America, rendered the policy of wooing China from Russia virtually impossible. The United States did not abandon all plans to impair the Sino-Soviet alliance, however; it radically altered its tactics. Thenceforth, the United States sought to weaken the alliance by pressing China economically, diplomatically, and militarily, forcing it to make demands of the Soviet Union that were imprudent or otherwise impossible for Moscow to meet. Unrelenting pressure on the alliance was designed essentially to disrupt it. American strategy in the 1954–1955 offshore islands crisis, for example, involved more than protection of an ally's security and status. The United States exploited the crisis as part of a broader general scheme, premised on pressure toward China, which was increased at each opportunity. This overall American approach to the Sino-Soviet alliance was reasonably effective and suited to the public mood.

Pure policy, of course, is never executed, and simple, unqualified explanations are inadequate for understanding problems in international relations. My study of this problem has resulted in a complicated, not especially tidy, interpretation of American policy. Plans, perceptions, contingencies, domestic politics, the quality of Sino-Soviet relations at a given time, and particular personalities influenced American diplomacy. Determining the mix and measuring the results—intended and otherwise—have been central problems. The continued unavailability of certain pertinent documents, especially from 1953 to 1955, has hindered the tracing of different lines of American policy thinking, explanations of why one strategy was selected over another, and estimates of the overall effectiveness of Washington's policy; nevertheless, declassified material now in the public domain strongly supports and indeed forms the backbone of the approach taken here.[7]

Use of the term ''alliance'' and problems of periodization raise immediate

6. Dean Acheson, *Present at the Creation* (New York, 1969), 481.
7. Unfortunately, volume XIV of the *Foreign Relations of the United States, 1952–1954* (Washington, 1985) appeared too late for use in this book; nonetheless, many of the declassified

issues and preliminary questions. Throughout most of 1949, the Soviet Union formally recognized the authority of its 1945 treaty with China, pledging Moscow to security cooperation with the non-Marxist regime of Chiang Kai-shek. Almost to the very end of the Chinese civil war on the mainland, Moscow accredited its ambassador to the Nationalist government. But it is the character of Soviet-Chinese party relations in 1949, rather than the government-to-government relations of Russia and China, on which I will first concentrate. Not until early 1950, after the Chinese Communist party assumed state power and Mao Tse-tung journeyed to Moscow, did the Sino-Soviet alliance with which this study is concerned emerge, publicly heralded by communists around the world. Furthermore, as will soon be apparent, an important distinction must be recognized between the formal-legal aspects of the Sino-Soviet partnership and its true nature, which is not wholly conveyed by any conventional understanding of "alliance." The term is thus employed only modestly and partly for convenience. And yet during the period studied here, Russians, Chinese, and Americans did acknowledge a Sino-Soviet combination of some sort, which was opposed to the United States.[8] On this last point more will be said later.

The second problem can be phrased as follows: why does the period from 1949 to 1955 constitute an identifiable chapter in Sino-Soviet-American history? Allowing for the provisional and essentially subjective nature of periodization, a study of American policy toward the socialist alliance during this period makes sense, both in the context of post–World War II Communist-American rivalry and of Sino-Soviet relations since 1949.

COMMUNIST-AMERICAN RIVALRY

The Soviet-American wartime partnership of 1941 to 1945 was based solely on the mutual desire to destroy Nazi Germany. Suspicion rooted in ideological antipathy and historical conflict underlay Washington's necessary alli-

---

documents appearing in volume XIV had been previously declassified and are cited in my notes. Most of the material contained in the new *FRUS* appears to support my interpretation and central thesis.

8. Robert Simmons, in *The Strained Alliance* (New York, 1975), attempts to develop a typology of ideal alliance forms and contrasts a "partnership-alliance" with a "protectorate-alliance." His effort—in an otherwise excellent book—is marred by uncertainty about his own categories. For example, in trying to illuminate the nature of a protectorate-alliance, he is vague and confusing, saying that it thrives "when there is a symmetry in the expenditure of each [country] of similarly treasured core values." Whatever else Simmons has in mind, this statement is an example of scholarship stymied by jargon. I will avoid elaborate definitions of "alliance" and instead will try to illustrate the inflections of Sino-Soviet relations between 1949 and 1955.

ance with Moscow. During the Russian civil war the United States had actually intervened against the Bolshevik regime, and not until 1933 did the American government officially recognize Moscow. Comintern activity in the United States, though largely ineffective, convincingly revealed Soviet hostility in the 1920s and 1930s. Not surprisingly, then, despite collaboration in the struggle against Germany, the Grand Alliance broke when its raison d'être ended. By 1947, however, the nature of Soviet-American antagonism, previously never a threat to global stability, had altered; indeed, the entire international order had been transformed. Europe was devastated, and the local states could no longer maintain the traditional balance of forces. Germany was ruined and occupied, France was demoralized, and an enfeebled Great Britain had begun to liquidate its empire.

After the war, the Soviet regime sought means to assure external security and avoid future disasters. For Joseph Stalin, idealistic principles of world peace embodied in the American-inspired United Nations Charter could not substitute for "friendly" (essentially Soviet-controlled) governments on Russia's vulnerable western frontier. Stalin soon grew suspicious of the American-designed, universally pretentious collective security system and viewed it as a mere tool of American diplomacy. Meanwhile, he forced subservient regimes upon those central and east European states occupied by the Red Army. Perceived Soviet security needs, requiring specific regional arrangements, resulted hence in a new communist *cordon sanitaire*.

The American administration, hoping to prolong postwar Allied cooperation, did not react as decisively to the Grand Alliance's collapse as Winston Churchill would have liked. But by 1947, the United States had abandoned the chimera of Soviet-American peacetime partnership and assumed the role in Europe traditionally played by Great Britain. The Continent's strategic balance, threatened by the Soviet Union, was sustained by massive American economic and military aid.

Clashing concepts of security and interest had by 1949 displaced wartime hopes for durable Allied concert. A historically unique, politically symmetrical division of Europe took root. The several lesser states on either side coalesced around a power center and adopted—or had imposed on them—its form of social-political organization. Militarization of the bipolar scheme ensued, and confrontation in Europe expanded into Soviet-American rivalry over other parts of the world, notably China, Korea, and the Middle East.

The Korean armistice, the 1954 Geneva Conference on Southeast Asia, and the East-West summit meeting in 1955 marked the beginning of Soviet and American attempts to ameliorate major problems. Afterward, Soviet and American leaders groped persistently toward the minimal diplomatic object: avoidance of war. Berlin 1958, Cuba 1962, and the October, 1973, American "alert" indicated the depth of constant mutual suspicion and antagonism. Yet limited cooperation in achieving the minimal goal was maintained, finding tangible expression in the 1963 Test Ban Treaty and in the strategic arms limitation negotiations and agreements of the 1970s.

The period 1949–1955 also marks a distinct phase in the history of Sino-American relations. At the beginning of this time the United States faced the vexing problem of how to deal with a unified China whose leaders had toppled a wartime ally of Washington's, professed an ideology hostile to the West, and were associated with Russia. The frozen status of Sino-American diplomatic relations that obtained for nearly a generation was not finally, definitely fixed until the end of 1955. As late as 1955—despite Chinese-American fighting in Korea, UN condemnation of China, and the embargo—the American government still considered the possibility of formal, if limited, intercourse with China. Two decades then elapsed before Sino-American relations were substantially improved and expanded.

SINO-SOVIET RELATIONS

Sino-Soviet relations since 1949 have been characterized by extreme differences in cultural-political heritage, revolutionary experience, and, most important, uneven levels of technological-industrial development—all factors conducive to conflict. Amid the causes, evident even between 1949 and 1955, directly attributable to the rift, none are so prominent as the divergence of security interests and rivalry, at first latent, for authoritative position within the communist movement. From these two problems the other issues of dispute have evolved. At first aggravating security policy disagreements and inciting leadership rivalry, acerbic debate and differences both in domestic policies and among personalities gained independent momentum and became in themselves divisive issues. In turn, they later spawned new problems such as a serious border dispute and sharp, albeit limited, armed fighting. Alleged devotion to a common ideology also caused both sides to view the divergence of national interests with a sense of betrayal, ever deepening as the "partnership" deteriorated.

Between 1949 and 1955, however, the two states, on the basis of assumed ideological compatibility and a perceived American threat, combined in formal alliance. This period is regarded by analysts—Donald Zagoria, William Griffith, Harold Hinton, and Chinese and Soviet commentators—as the period of greatest intracommunist cooperation.[9] According to all of them, important Sino-Soviet differences began only with the Twentieth Congress of the Soviet Communist party in 1956. As China's leaders repeatedly liked to declare: "The Twentieth Congress of the CPSU was the first step along the road of revisionism taken by the leadership of the CPSU. From the Twentieth Congress to the present, the revisionist line of the CPSU has gone through the process of emergence, formation, growth and systemization."[10] Yet contrary to such official Chinese statements, serious problems plagued the friendship even during the era of closest Sino-Soviet collaboration.

In summation, this book deals with the period of acute Soviet-American antagonism followed by the beginning of Cold War thaw and the time, generally agreed upon by scholars and actors alike, as the peak period in Peking-Moscow relations. By 1956, partly as a consequence of improved Soviet-American relations, strains had developed within the communist alliance, imperiling its vigor.

9. For a fuller explanation of this view consult William Griffith, *The Sino-Soviet Rift* (London, 1964); O. B. Borisov and B. T. Koloskov, *Sino-Soviet Relations, 1945–1973* (Moscow, 1975); Harold Hinton, *China's Turbulent Quest* (Bloomington, 1972); Alfred Low, *The Sino-Soviet Dispute* (London, 1976); G. F. Hudson, Richard Lowenthal, and Roderick MacFarquhar, *The Sino-Soviet Dispute* (New York, 1961); and Donald Zagoria, *The Sino-Soviet Conflict, 1956–1961* (New York, 1973).

10. *People's Daily*, September 6, 1963.

Chapter I

AMERICA'S RESPONSE TO COMMUNIST VICTORIES 1947–1948

Marxist agitation in China began in earnest in the 1920s, and over the years tensions developed between the Soviet and Chinese Communist parties. Apparent Soviet-Chinese party cooperation by the late 1940s veiled past antagonisms and latent suspicions. Most American policy makers were aware of these problems in 1947 and 1948 and devised their strategy accordingly, at the same time bracing themselves for a spectacular communist victory in China.

SOVIET-CHINESE PARTY RELATIONS

Through the apparatus of the Third International, Soviet leaders attempted to dictate the strategy and, to a lesser degree, the short-range goals of China's Communist party (CCP). Comintern advocacy of socialist cooperation with Chiang Kai-shek's Kuomintang (KMT) army against different warlords and later the Japanese invaders caused severe setbacks for the Communist party and army in 1927.

The initial, utterly disastrous phase of Soviet-Comintern guidance partly reflected the contest for power in Moscow between Stalin and Leon Trotsky. Beginning in 1925, at least according to his memoirs, Trotsky demanded communist withdrawal from the Kuomintang and warned that excessively close CCP-Chiang relations threatened Chinese communist safety and revolutionary integrity. Stalin urged instead, however, that isolated, vulnerable Russia cultivate a stable Chinese state as a buffer against possible renewed

Japanese and British adventures. By 1926, Chiang seemed likely to unify his country and violently opposed any British and Japanese designs on it. In Stalin's view, Chiang was therefore in a better position to advance Soviet Far Eastern security than were the scattered, significantly weaker Chinese Marxists. This position was justified ideologically by the claim that, until the proletariat was both more numerous and politically sophisticated, the CCP should support the bourgeois national revolution. Orthodox Marxist reasoning prevailed and was incorporated into a September, 1926, Soviet Central Committee resolution, which charged Stalin's domestic opponents and some increasingly apprehensive Chinese colleagues with uncritical, un-Marxist thinking. They were held to be "completely incorrect" to believe that the liberation struggle in feudal China could proceed without the aid of the progressive and patriotic elements in the bourgeoisie, which were concentrated in the Kuomintang. Only after the successful completion of the bourgeois-democratic revolution, warned the Central Committee, should the CCP and the Chinese proletariat inaugurate a socialist struggle.

In the spring of 1927, the Kuomintang army, without warning, turned upon its nominal ally and liquidated thousands of communist cadres and soldiers. In Shanghai the workers' movement was ruthlessly suppressed; casualties among the proletariat, whether communist or not, were staggering. Following the debacle, Stalin sought Chinese scapegoats. Mao was singled out and heavily criticized by the Moscow-approved CCP elite. The struggle against Trotsky, even though near its fateful climax, did not allow admitting mistakes.

Trotsky, essentially defeated by Stalin by 1927, produced years later in his memoirs a scathing indictment of Stalin's "criminal," bungling handling of the affair: "The policy of Stalin . . . not only prepared for and facilitated the crushing of the revolution but, with the help of reprisals by the state apparatus, shielded the counter-revolutionary work of Chiang Kai-shek and called for confidence in him. Chiang drowned the Shanghai workers and the Communist party in blood."[1] Thus depicted, Stalin's unscientific judgments and stupidity made him indeed the "gravedigger" of revolution. Actually, though, to the degree that Trotsky even thought about Chinese events in the early 1920s—until 1927 he was largely indifferent—he tended to agree with Stalin's assessment. He felt that threats posed by the British Empire, still capitalist enemy number one, and imperial Japan mattered more in determining

1. Leon Trotsky, *My Life* (New York, 1970), 529–30.

Soviet Far Eastern interests than the fate of a bunch of Chinese revolutionary novitiates. Trotsky especially feared that Great Britain and Japan might compose their differences and make common cause against the Soviet Union. He consequently favored playing the two powers off against each other and at one point thought to placate Tokyo by giving Japan a free hand in Manchuria, a galling suggestion to all Chinese whatever their political party allegiance. Trotsky did not oppose CCP subordination to the Kuomintang until very late, after it was obvious, except perhaps to Stalin, that the two parties were bound to collide. Moreover, Trotsky offered not the slightest objection when in 1926 the Kuomintang was admitted to the Comintern as a "sympathizing party." He was realistic and cold-blooded enough to recognize that "one can have an alliance with the Kuomintang, but an ally has to be watched just like an enemy."[2] But Trotsky's much-touted prescience was, like Stalin's, not keen enough, nor forcefully enough backed, to warn the Comintern against disasters in Shanghai and Hunan.

Official Soviet versions of early Russian-Chinese party relations naturally entirely oppose Trotsky's. According to Soviet historians, for example O. B. Borisov and B. T. Koloskov, Chiang scored successes against the CCP because China's social nature—semicolonial, feudal, and economically, culturally, and politically backward—was too undeveloped to support a successful proletarian revolution. In their view, the Marxist-international element of the CCP was tragically destroyed in 1927 while heroically resisting Chiang's treachery; only the perfidious, national petit-bourgeois group survived, thus dooming China's revolution to an ignominious non-Marxist fate.[3] Soviet historians are also reticent about Comintern activities in China and in any case do not ascribe blame to the International. Borisov and Koloskov fail even to mention the names of Soviet agents in China, let alone their advice, foolish or not. Such future PRC leaders as Kang Sheng are mentioned by the Russian writers and implicated in Kuomintang victories.

Although Chinese statements concerning Soviet-Comintern assistance during the 1920s have been only mildly critical, they do reveal early problems and doubts about Moscow's wisdom and suggest later resentments. Mao once reported that Michael Borodin, who made intelligence assessments for Stalin and delivered his instructions to CCP leaders, was a blunderer.[4] More telling still is a *People's Daily* editorial written in 1963, championing Stalin

2. Adam Ulam, *Expansion and Coexistence* (New York, 1969), 178.
3. Borisov and Koloskov, *Sino-Soviet Relations*, 100.
4. Klaus Mehnert, *Peking and Moscow* (New York, 1963), 240.

against Nikita Khrushchev's accusations. Within the context of apology are the following remarks: "Long ago the Chinese Communists had first hand experience of some of Stalin's mistakes. Of the erroneous 'Left' and 'Right' opportunist lines which emerged in the Chinese Communist Party at one time or another, some arose under the influence of certain mistakes of Stalin's."[5] The editorial went on to explain how Mao from the late 1920s through the 1940s successfully resisted Stalin's poor advice.

In the early 1930s, a murky period in CCP-CPSU relations, Marxist leader Li Li-san complained of mutual distrust between Russian and Chinese comrades. It is small wonder why. Stalin, far from the scene and lacking even intuitive insight, continued to direct, as best he could, Chinese Marxist policy. Intense competition meanwhile developed between the Moscow-trained, Moscow-indebted "Returned Students" faction of the CCP and the indigenous elite, exemplified by Mao. One of the unintended but patently good effects from Mao's point of view of Chiang's annihilation campaigns was that during the Long March CCP-Moscow contact was severely limited. From this period onward and culminating at Yenan, Mao consolidated his party power, gained experience in political administration, and undertook revolutionary experiments—he adapted Russian theories to Chinese conditions.

The Soviet-inspired united front of the later 1930s gave rise to an uneasy alliance between Kuomintang and communists against Japan. Initially, the rival Chinese parties managed a limited cooperative war against the Japanese, but by 1939 fighting between the KMT and People's Liberation Army (PLA) nearly ruptured the alliance, and it dissolved into a mere "armed truce." Mao capitalized on the war by expanding the territory and population under Marxist control. According to American intelligence, the communists governed 1.5 million people and 35,000 square miles in 1937. By 1945, the CCP ruled 85 million people in an area of 225,000 square miles.[6] Chiang, less interested in fighting the Japanese than in preparing for a showdown with his domestic opponents, also maneuvered to improve his geographical and military position. By 1944, while the Americans carried the brunt of the war against Japan, the two Chinese parties were virtually engaged in a war within the war, which led ultimately to Mao's victory in 1949. Before his triumph, though, the Americans tried to bolster Chiang's security by promoting a Sino-Soviet

    5. *People's Daily*, September 13, 1963, quoted in John Gittings, *Survey of the Sino-Soviet Dispute* (London, 1968), 42.
    6. Robert North, *Moscow and the Chinese Communists* (Stanford, 1963), 206.

friendship treaty (1945), and later in the civil war they worked to negotiate a domestic peace through General George Marshall.

During the civil war, Soviet leaders seem to have been skeptical of CCP strength and warned against a direct frontal assault on the Chinese republic. Evidence of preliberation Russian-Chinese party disquiet comes from Stalin himself, who once reportedly remarked to the Yugoslav communist Milovan Djilas: "True, we, too, can make a mistake! Here, when the war with Japan ended, we invited the Chinese comrades to reach an agreement as to how a modus vivendi with Chiang Kai-shek might be found. They agreed with us in word, but in deed they did it their own way when they got home: they mustered their forces and struck . . . they were right and not we."[7]

Stalin's support of the CCP in the late 1940s was nominal, and, as noted previously, he even signed a mutual security pact with the Nationalist government. Fearful of America's growing military strength in Asia after the war, Stalin followed a cautious policy toward China lest he antagonize Chiang by too openly supporting the communists, thereby forcing him to seek decisive American intervention. Not until Mao achieved total control of the mainland and the possibility of massive American aid to the Nationalists completely dissipated did the Soviet Union formally recognize the Chinese communist regime. Until then, the Soviet government's correct diplomatic relations with Chiang must have piqued Mao.

More disturbing to CCP leaders than Moscow's excessive consideration for the class enemy were cases in 1946 of Red Army misdeeds in Manchuria. These included abuse of the population and wholesale removal of Chinese industrial plants and machinery to Russian territory. Normally very favorably disposed toward the Soviets, Li Li-san admitted to a Western journalist in 1946 that "there were instances of faulty Soviet behavior in Manchuria."[8] And yet there is reason to believe that the Red Army's presence and transfer of captured Japanese weapons to Lin Piao's forces strengthened the PLA's Manchurian position during the civil war.

Despite Mao's self-proclaimed adherence to the principle of Soviet leadership, the CCP's discreet distance in the late 1930s and cautious disobedience in the 1940s—leading to victory—indirectly threatened Moscow's socialist leadership. The allegedly wiser, revolution-tested Kremlin men also confronted ideological competition in the thought of Mao Tse-tung. At the CCP's Seventh Party Congress in April, 1945, Mao was credited with qual-

7. Milovan Djilas, *Conversations with Stalin* (New York, 1962), 182.
8. Gittings, *Survey of the Sino-Soviet Dispute*, 11.

ities of doctrinal originality and genius. Even earlier, during the 1930s, Mao had claimed that China's revolution would serve as a model for all other colonial and semicolonial countries. Implicit in such an assertion was the primacy of China's revolution and leadership over Russia's, at least for most of Asia and Africa. Shortly after liberation, Peking spokesmen made similar pronouncements, which were alarming to Soviet sensibilities.

Fulfillment of Lenin's historic ambition, a red China, was not enthusiastically greeted in the Soviet Union. Stalin was disturbed and preoccupied by a renegade Tito, and his anxiety over Soviet "proletarian leadership" was quickened by the emergence of a socialist China. By late 1948, events demonstrated that Soviet control over Eastern Europe—except, obviously, Yugoslavia—was nearly absolute. China, however, was unoccupied by Soviet troops, and its popular-based party had gained power by its own effort. Mao himself had declared in a 1936 interview with Edgar Snow that the Chinese communists were "certainly not fighting for an emancipated China in order to turn the country over to Moscow!"[9]

Nevertheless, fourteen years later, Mao's China, devoted to revolution, was under Stalin's tutelage, allied to Russia, and committed to friendship and mutual assistance. To millions of people throughout the world, whether or not they applauded, it seemed clear that the West had been routed in Asia and that international communism had won its greatest victory since 1917.

AMERICA'S RESPONSE

Most American policy makers were sorely disappointed upon realizing that new, unified China, increasingly stable, could not be relied upon to support American interests in the Far East. Not only were Washington's long-standing hopes for an ally in China extinguished, but Mao's ideological and diplomatic links to the Soviet Union seemed to portend dark, gloomy reverses ahead. A Joint Strategic Survey Committee report ruefully acknowledged in 1949 that there was an "enormous differential, strategically speaking, between a friendly and a Soviet-controlled or Soviet-allied China."[10]

One official, the talented chief of the State Department's Policy Planning Staff (PPS), George Kennan, did hold the opinion that China's military significance was not so great and that Moscow would not immediately reap huge advantages through alliance with Peking. He wrote in September, 1948, that

9. Quoted in Stuart Schram, *The Political Thought of Mao Tse-Tung* (New York, 1969), 419.
10. Joint Strategic Survey Committee Memorandum to Joint Chiefs of Staff, 1721/30, Record Group 218, National Archives, Washington, D.C. (hereafter RG, NA).

China's limited industrial development, vast social and economic problems, and the poor leadership and training of its army greatly qualified the country's potential usefulness as an ally in the event of war, whether aligned with the United States or Russia: "Until China develops a modern transportation network in its vast hinterland it will, excepting for its coastal fringe, more closely resemble a strategic morass than a strategic springboard."[11]

However unimpressed they were by China's military weight, Kennan and the Policy Planning Staff were moved to report that Moscow's struggle for the allegiance of China's millions was disturbing because a communist victory there would profoundly embarrass the West. The staff also recognized that "China is worth having because capture of it would represent an impressive political victory and, more practically, acquisition of a broad human glacis from which to mount a political offensive against the rest of East Asia."[12] Indeed, by the end of 1949, Moscow's influence in one form or another stretched from the Baltic to the East China Sea.

Neither American nor British leaders were prepared to acquiesce to possible Soviet control in the Far East. And they were determined, before and after Mao's victory, to diminish Soviet sway in Peking. State Department officials, namely Kennan and members of his staff, began developing contingency plans as early as 1947. Unprecedented problems within the Soviet bloc in Eastern Europe also encouraged American policy makers dealing with China.

Through 1947 and 1948, neither American diplomats nor the intelligence services determined with certainty the type and amount of Soviet aid proffered to the Chinese communists. Kuomintang evidence of alleged massive Russian supplies to the People's Liberation Army was spotty and failed to convince either American soldiers or embassy staff. Except for the Soviet delivery of captured Japanese arms (one historian, Robert Simmons, speculates that these weapons were only grudgingly handed over to the PLA or perhaps snatched by Lin Piao's men), direct Soviet aid was never clearly established, and its importance was therefore doubted by most Western observers. The great bulk of captured PLA weapons, in fact, bore American serial numbers.

Wanton Soviet misbehavior and destructiveness in Manchuria were understood at the State Department as repugnant to the local population and the CCP. At the time, U.S. officials in China estimated that the value of Soviet-

11. PPS/39, September 7, 1948, in Anna Nelson (ed.), *The State Department Policy Planning Staff Papers, 1947–1949* (3 vols., New York, 1983), II, 412–46.
12. *Ibid.*

caused damage and expropriations exceeded $885,100,000. Walton Butterworth, minister-counsel of the American embassy, wrote of Soviet conduct in Manchuria: "They tore it down and left, not even permitting the Chinese Communists to come in until they had themselves evacuated. The result has been that the Manchurian people have a hatred for the Russians which is so great it almost has to be experienced personally to be believed."[13] He explained further that because of Manchuria, Soviet prestige had fallen throughout Asia, complicating future Soviet relations with China, whether ruled by communists or not. Butterworth also noted that Soviet influence, let alone control, over the PLA campaign renewed in January, 1947, was slight. In a cable written several months later, Consul General Edmund Clubb repeated Butterworth's points on Soviet misdeeds and asserted that Soviet aid for the PLA was minuscule. He also noted pervasive reports of a division within the CCP. Clubb believed that Mao, representing Marxist nationalists, and Li Lisan, formerly head of the party and recently returned from Moscow after fourteen years, were bitterly opposed to each other. The clash between personalities and leadership rivalry, he contended, stemmed mainly from Mao's hostility to any foreign influences, including Soviet.[14] Yet neither Clubb nor Butterworth doubted overall CCP affinity for the Soviet Union, and both recognized that inspiration, if not dependable support, came from Moscow.

Angus Ward, American consul general in Mukden, disagreed with his two colleagues' assessments of Soviet influence. Amid a December, 1947, communist offensive in Manchuria, he reported that Soviet materiel aid to the PLA was substantial but well concealed. Ward predicted that following communist victory the Soviets would replace with their own creatures, as they had in Eastern Europe, those Chinese leaders impervious to Moscow's will.[15]

Clubb's and Butterworth's analyses, not Ward's, were reviewed with approval by the State Department's Policy Planning Staff. John Paton Davies, PPS expert on China and a man deeply admired by Kennan, believed from the outset that the Russians and Chinese were inevitable adversaries. Davies thought that the United States had only to avoid making itself an enemy of the CCP. If America were correct in its dealings with China, bad relations between the mainland states would develop naturally, and the United States would then be in an excellent position to salvage something of its interest and

13. U.S. Department of State, *Foreign Relations of the United States, 1947* (Washington, D.C., 1972), VII, 9, (hereafter *FRUS*).
14. *Ibid.*, 337.
15. *Ibid.*, 401.

prestige in China. Davies' analysis persuaded Kennan and through him influenced Secretary Marshall and later Dean Acheson.

In a lecture at the National War College delivered just one day after formal establishment of the Policy Planning Staff (May 5, 1947), Kennan revealed his and Davies' understanding—soon to become basic PPS doctrine—of Soviet possibilities in China. He argued that the Russians were not well equipped to manage Chinese nationalism, in communist guise or any other, and that the CCP was not a reliable, long-term subordinate to Moscow: "As long as the Chinese Communists remain a little minority movement fighting for their lives . . . they have to keep on fairly good terms with Moscow. If they were to come to control, let's say, a large portion of the territory of China, I am not sure their relations with Moscow would be much different from those of Chiang today, because they would be much more independent, much more in a position to take an independent line vis-a-vis Moscow." [16]

However sound such an interpretation may have been and however convinced some men in the administration were by it, it could hardly placate Congress or the nation at large as China, or a large chunk of it, passed into the communist camp. The administration was in an awkward bind. It was simultaneously trying to avoid burdensome commitments to Chiang, appease right-wing domestic critics, and bolster bipartisan support for its foreign policy.

Shortly after his return from China, newly appointed Secretary of State George Marshall confronted these problems in testifying in February, 1947, before the Senate Foreign Relations Committee. Marshall opposed granting the request of Dr. T. V. Soong, director of the Executive Yuan, for an American loan of $150–250 million, supposedly to purchase cotton. Marshall urged that, instead, the United Nations Relief and Rehabilitation Administration should be pressed to supply the needed commodity; he hoped such action would produce "a helpful effect without just pouring money down a rat hole." And based on the cotton issue, Marshall drew broader conclusions: "We must never just give them money. It must be a very controlled matter. It has to be, every bit of it. But the question now is whether you can even do that with any prospect of a definite return." [17]

Thoroughly pessimistic about the Chinese government's prospects, Marshall also opposed American military intervention. A soldier of vast experi-

16. George Kennan, *Memoirs, 1925–1950* (Boston, 1967), 374.

17. *Executive Sessions of the Senate Foreign Relations Committee* (Washington, D.C., 1976), I, 4.

ence and prestige, he insisted that the communists were masters of guerrilla warfare, were imbued with zeal, and could endure far more than ordinary fighting men; by contrast, Nationalist forces were demoralized, their lines of communication were under continuous harassment, and the countryside was lost. The secretary dismissed Chiang's prediction that victory could be won in six to eight months. As for Soviet-CCP relations, Marshall confirmed the latter's ideological purity and sympathy for Moscow. But he distinguished between the two communist parties and declared that the Chinese were not subservient. Rather, unlike the corrupt, graft-plagued government, they were determined to salvage their country through strict, moral, independent discipline.

During the same period as Marshall's testimony, an unpropitious event occurred that, although modest in itself, foreshadowed the impending tempest that later wreaked havoc upon American policy in Asia. The Senate in early winter 1947 began to consider Truman's nomination of John Carter Vincent as career minister. His nomination had been submitted along with those of nine other foreign service officers, all of whom were routinely approved, but Vincent's promotion was not secured until April. On January 23, Senator Styles Bridges had requested a delay of Vincent's nomination so as to examine his case more closely. Bridges had apparently come to doubt Vincent's fitness for the post because of ''extensive facts and documentations'' provided by William Loeb, publisher of the Burlington, Vermont, *Daily News*. According to Loeb's independent investigation, Vincent's previous administration of the State Department's Far Eastern Division had been inspired by two communist texts, *The Program of the Communist International and Its Constitution* (1928) and *The Revolutionary Movement in the Colonies and Semi-Colonies* (1928).[18] Since 1941, Vincent was alleged to have attempted to sabotage Washington's China policy; misled his superiors; conspired with the likes of the ''unpatriotic'' Asian expert, Owen Lattimore; and thwarted the efforts of America's former ambassador to China, General Patrick Hurley. (Hurley, appointed by President Franklin Roosevelt, brought to his job remarkably little diplomatic skill or understanding of Chinese politics. He tended to blame his failures in China during World War II on his expert but hapless staff.)

In response to the charges, Acting Secretary of State Acheson championed Vincent, whom he described as ''a gentleman and a disinterested and loyal

18. *Ibid.*, 312.

servant of our republic.''[19] Acheson's impressive count-by-count refutation of unsubstantiated charges cleared his subordinate. Eventually, however, both Acheson and Marshall were to endure similar rough treatment.

In 1948, as communist forces in Manchuria began a series of campaigns isolating Nationalist armies in Changchun, Mukden, and Chinchow, Congress considered the merits of renewed assistance to China. Many congressional leaders believed that as prerequisite to additional aid for his regime, Chiang should adopt a series of domestic reforms aimed at eventually eradicating corruption, fairly distributing land, and promoting democracy, thereby expanding the base of his popular support against the communists. To Kennan, the congressional deliberations and sporadic attempts to force reforms on the Nationalist government were entirely beside the point. In what must be one of the most vigorous statements favoring a realpolitik ever uttered by an American policy maker, Kennan preached:

> We should stop putting ourselves in the position of being our brother's keeper and refrain from offering moral and ideological advice. We should cease to talk about vague and—for the Far East—unreal objectives such as human rights, the raising of the living standards, and democratization. The day is not far off when we are going to have to deal in straight power concepts. The less we are then hampered by idealistic slogans the better.[20]

Although the administration did not entirely give up on ''saving'' China until October, 1948, by February Kennan already had. He counseled ending American commitments to Chiang, thereby recovering detachment and maneuverability toward China, and boosting Philippine and Japanese security. He argued that the latter's obvious economic and military potential, proven in World War II, was vital to America's Pacific interests and Far Eastern security. Quixotic, expensive ventures in China would only distract from urgent rebuilding in Japan. Resistance to some of Kennan's suggestions came from members of the National Security Council (NSC). In March, the council considered Chinese difficulties and tried to assess how their conceivable resolution might affect the Soviet-American power balance. In doing so, the

19. *Ibid.*, 315.
20. Anna Nelson (ed.), *The Policy Planning Staff Papers, 1948* (New York, 1983), 122; PPS 23, February 24, 1948.

council confronted the ideas and perceptions of various government agencies and revealed within itself a range of opinion.[21]

The council readily acknowledged China's importance despite its small industrial plant, scarce natural resources, and widespread poverty. Given its geographical position and enormous manpower, a communist China would eventually strengthen Marxist revolutionary movements in Burma and Indochina; conversely, a unified China, independent and friendly to the United States, would be an asset in containing Soviet influence in East Asia. In case of Soviet-American war, a sympathetic China could also provide the United States with advanced bomber bases, extensive areas for army escape and evasion tactics, and the cooperation or at least benign neutrality of China's military.[22]

The NSC also judged that prospects for a CCP-KMT compromise remained dim. The Nationalist position was deemed desperate, and only substantial internal reforms and steady injections of foreign aid could preserve at most a truncated China for the West. At the same time, Soviet assistance to the CCP was recognized as thin, notwithstanding Moscow's sympathies for the rebels. The NSC speculated that as long as the Chinese communists continued to succeed, the Soviets would withhold costly help; but if American assistance resulted in communist reverses, the Soviets might resupply and openly encourage Mao.

The council then considered four hypothetical U.S. courses of action in support of the modest, immediate goal of saving at least part of China from communist domination. First, the United States could refrain from providing any more economic and military assistance. This action would most likely lead to prompt Nationalist collapse and communist consolidation of power. And although such a policy would free limited resources to areas of greater strategic significance than China, Europe in particular, the NSC admitted that refusal of additional aid would run counter to popular sentiments in America, which favored some form of U.S. commitment to China.

21. In November, 1947, Kennan recommended that the United States deliver aid to Chiang. Kennan, however, meant the aid primarily as a sop to domestic opinion: minimum aid would satisfy most of the American public and prevent a sudden collapse of the Chinese Republic. See Warren Cohen, "Acheson, His Advisors, and China," in Dorothy Borg and Waldo Heinrichs (eds.), *Uncertain Years: Chinese-American Relations, 1947–1950* (New York, 1980), 15. The National Security Council, approved by Congress on July 26, 1947, originally consisted of President Truman, Secretary of State Marshall, Secretary of Defense James Forrestal, Secretary of Army Kenneth Royall, Secretary of Navy John Sullivan, Secretary of Air Force W. Stuart Symington, and National Security Resources Board Director Arthur Hill.

22. NSC 6, March, 1948, NSC File, Modern Military Branch, NA.

The second option, the opposite policy, would assure all the economic and military help needed for securing Nationalist victory. The sheer magnitude of guaranteeing Nationalist success, however, defied reasonable calculation and risk. The NSC assumed that, in addition to delivering massive assistance, the United States would virtually have to administer China's government and underwrite its economy. Once the U.S. was committed to saving Chiang, withdrawal, for whatever reason, would be nearly impossible and resources soon depleted. American aid on such a scale might also precipitate large deliveries of Soviet equipment to the CCP, perhaps even leading to general war.

Lying between the extreme possibilities were two moderate proposals. Defense Department representatives James Forrestal, Kenneth Royall, John Sullivan, and W. Stuart Symington favored furnishing fair amounts of economic aid and some direct military assistance. Secretary Marshall and Arthur Hill from the National Security Resources Board voiced objections to this approach, however, and urged instead that the United States grant *only* economic help. The political-military division was not great, but it reflected differences of proportion and emphasis. Both groups agreed that China was of secondary strategic importance and that an exhausting American effort there should be avoided. Both claimed, too, that limited aid—whether economic and military or only economic—would at most delay Nationalist defeat but could not possibly guarantee victory; that decision ultimately lay with the Chinese alone. Yet by "buying time," declared Secretary Marshall, Chiang could institute the social reforms necessary if his army and cause were to flourish. To this counsel, Marshall and Hill added their concern that limited military aid might represent an obligation to Chiang from which it would be impossible to disengage and would likely form the basis of greater American responsibilities. Echoing Kennan, they warned that increased entanglement would compromise Washington's freedom of action in China and around the world. The defense secretaries, by contrast, worried less about Chinese internal reforms and the possibility of disastrous escalation. They recommended military assistance consisting of advisers and a large transfer of arms to Chiang; otherwise, immediate and total communist victory was inevitable. The service representatives also qualified the relegation of China to secondary status by claiming that a communist victory there would be highly unfavorable to Western prestige and strategic interests. In any case, they argued, only after moderate security was established should Chiang turn to admittedly serious social problems, thereby strengthening his overall position.[23]

23. *Ibid.*

The administration endorsed the State Department's recommendation to grant limited financial aid, enough to slow the rate of economic deterioration and enable the Chinese government to purchase, in either Europe or America, needed arms and supplies. Adopted by Congress in April, the China Aid Act appropriated $275 million for agricultural-industrial reconstruction and inflation control and tagged $125 million for military purchases. In view of the Nationalist position, the aid act, effective for only one year, was meager and incommensurate with its lofty ideal: ''to maintain the genuine independence and administrative integrity of China and to sustain and strengthen the principles of individual liberty and free institutions in China.'' [24]

The administration was understandably loath to become deeply involved with the losing side during a protracted war in a secondary theater. The aid package was aptly characterized from the administration's point of view by Truman ally Senator Arthur Vandenberg as ''the best plan or device we could bring about . . . to extend aid to China, without making hard and fast commitments which we did not feel it was wise to make.'' [25] The gap thus widened between China policy intent and public rhetoric.

President Truman, scarcely sanguine about Chiang's prospects, did try to distinguish for Congress's benefit the administration's generosity and concern for China from its problems of remaining noncommunist. In recommending the China legislation, he delivered the following caveats:

> We can assist in retarding the current economic deterioration and thus give the Chinese Government a further opportunity to initiate the measures necessary to the establishment of more stable economic conditions. But it is, and has been, clear that only the Chinese Government itself can undertake the vital measures necessary to provide the framework within which efforts toward peace and true economic recovery may be effective.

Truman also tried to impress upon his listeners that American assistance to Chiang was not even in small measure a substitute for the various social and democratic reforms that China had to undertake if it were successfully to resist communist subversion and conquest. [26]

The president neglected to say that as long as the United States refrained from directly relieving Chiang's severely pressed army, the possibilities for Nationalist-inspired economic and social reforms were extremely remote. But by its gestures the administration hoped to appease pro-China critics such as

24. Tang Tsou, *America's Failure in China* (Chicago, 1963), 475.
25. Vandenberg to Robert Lovett, April 6, 1948, Telegram #893.50/648, RG 59, NA.
26. *Congressional Record*, 80th Cong., 2nd sess., 1396.

Senator William Knowland, who, if left dissatisfied, threatened to campaign intensively against crucial European relief programs. Meanwhile, in southeastern Europe, events were taking an unexpected turn that directly began to influence State Department and NSC attitudes toward China.

In June, 1948, Yugoslavia broke with the Soviet Union and was expelled from the Cominform. Belgrade's leaders were excommunicated, condemned as heretics against the international faith. To the administration Yugoslav defiance of Moscow was especially welcome, for that drama raised the possibility of Soviet power receding from Eastern Europe. The National Security Council recorded hopefully, "The attitude we take now may constitute an important precedent." [27]

To the NSC, an enemy of America's chief adversary was not necessarily a friend. Yugoslav hostility—downing American airplanes, pressures on Trieste—and contempt for the capitalist West were plainly acknowledged. The council, reasonably, did not expect devoted Yugoslav communists, despite their poor relations with Russia, suddenly to embrace the United States. It was more likely, speculated the NSC, that both communist countries would try to patch up their differences for appearance's sake or perhaps attempt true reconciliation. Yet no matter how short-lived the Soviet-Yugoslav division, its effect would reverberate throughout the communist camp for years to come. Yugoslavia's opposition demonstrated that Russia could be successfully resisted. "The possibility of defection from Moscow, which has heretofore been unthinkable for foreign communist leaders, will from now on be present in one form or another in the mind of every one of them." [28]

The council feared that Western fawning on Tito might arouse feelings of revulsion within the Soviet bloc and among his followers, culminating in his overthrow and Yugoslavia's return to the Russian fold. Western and particularly American chilliness toward Belgrade, however, would dangerously aggravate Tito's sense of international isolation. Yugoslavia might then be held up as proof by Moscow that desertion from Soviet ranks left a socialist country at the mercy of capitalist wolves. The council therefore resolved in late June to adopt a cautious, moderate official attitude, neither incredulous and belligerent nor overly friendly. Tito's overtures would be carefully considered, but American initiatives would at first be reserved.

The council insisted on maintaining a public interpretation distinct from the concerns and goals privately expressed to foreign governments. The Ameri-

27. NSC 18, June 30, 1948, NSC File, Modern Military Branch, NA.
28. Ibid.

can public was warned not to expect much from Yugoslavia, a communist state and an implacable foe of democracy. At most, Yugoslav defiance demonstrated to all "non-Russian communists . . . that they have no future as the servants of Kremlin policies" and that totalitarianism, as before, could be defeated.[29] American diplomats were instructed to admit to other governments that internal Yugoslav politics mattered little so long as Belgrade was not a Soviet instrument.

Normal economic relations between the United States and various Western allies with Yugoslavia were encouraged, and regular trade soon revived. By the end of 1948, prohibitions on conventional munitions shipments were lifted and credits extended to Tito's government. A few years later, British, American, and French military leaders met with Yugoslav representatives to coordinate joint defense planning against Russia.

At the time the decision was made to expand economic and political relations with Belgrade, the administration felt obliged to defend its diplomacy against critics who would condemn American trade with any communist country. Kennan counseled: "We should explain that in exchange for goods of American origin we are receiving certain strategic mineral ores and concentrates which are of importance to the security of the United States, that this government does not like the present Yugoslav communist dictatorship and the relaxation of export controls in favor of Yugoslavia in no sense implies a desire to appease Tito nor does it signify approval of his regime."[30] American security, of course, hardly required Yugoslav-mined minerals and ores. Yet the administration felt compelled to justify for ostensible reasons of military preparedness a policy actually aimed at and based on national differences between two communist states. The myth that pernicious international communism—rather than the Soviet Union—threatened American security, institutions, and economy was thus not dispelled but indirectly was subtly strengthened.

Although lacking public candor, the administration obviously recognized that socialist uniformity faintly concealed national diversity and resolved in August that America's "first aim with respect to Russia in time of peace is to encourage and promote by means short of war the gradual retraction of undue Russian power and influence from the present satellite area and the emergence of the respective eastern European countries as independent factors on

29. Ibid.
30. NSC 20, July 12, 1948, ibid.

the international scene."[31] Although the desirability of socialist internal change was implied in this statement by the NSC (as in many others), the emphasis was strictly on prying satellite states loose from Soviet domination. Their independence would deprive Russia of manpower pools, natural resources, and abundant agricultural and industrial products.

In late summer of 1948, the United States began exploiting strains within the Soviet bloc by publicizing American economic might and its beneficial consequences, illustrated by the European Recovery Plan and a resuscitated Western Europe. Eventually, the promise of American generosity and the advantages of relations with her were paraded before the Chinese communists, too.

As far as Americans could tell, Chinese communist reaction to the Soviet-Yugoslav split was circumspect but not without interest. Mao, like most communist leaders, dutifully applauded Moscow's attempt to squelch heresy; he also chastised the recalcitrant Tito for treason. But below the surface, American observers suspected things were not so simple for Mao, and there was evidence that he was having difficulties of his own with Soviet loyalists in the CCP. Minister-Counselor Lewis Clark reported to Secretary Marshall on August 30 that apart from Mao's statement, Chinese communist propaganda had been conspicuously silent on the subject of Soviet-Yugoslav antagonism. He also reported that a communist spokesman in Hong Kong had told an American official that Mao's statement was ill-advised and that Yugoslavia's expulsion from the Cominform should be worrisome to the CCP leadership. Clark asserted, "Certainly there is no evidence as yet of an attempt by Chinese Communists to modify various lines of policy which have been similar to those for which Yugoslavia had been criticized in line with the Cominform statement." He speculated that this might be evidence of a deep rift between Mao Tse-tung and Li Li-san.[32]

One week later, the Policy Planning Staff submitted a report that noted Soviet attempts through Li Li-san to force the CCP to heed Moscow's discipline. Furthermore, Kennan and Davies commented that, although the Chinese communists had assumed suzerainty over Jehol Mongols, the Manchurian Mongols had been left alone, presumably in deference to Soviet wishes. The staff suspected the Soviets of encouraging separatist regimes in northern Manchuria and Sinkiang in hopes of bringing them under Moscow's direct rule. The Soviets were thought to desire retaining Chinese border provinces

31. NSC 20/1, August 18, 1948, *ibid.*
32. *FRUS, 1948* (Washington, D.C., 1973), VII, 442.

for military and economic purposes while maintaining decisive influence over a fragmented China. But why, since these areas were largely occupied by the People's Liberation Army, did the Soviets want to usurp the position of their Chinese comrades?

Kennan and his staff believed that Tito's truancy demonstrated for Moscow that ideology was not strong enough to bind foreign communists to Russia nor was it a substitute for Soviet control of a foreign state's party, secret police, and armed forces. These facts, Kennan explained, as applied to China, were as unsatisfactory to the Kremlin as they had been in the case of Yugoslavia. He believed that Moscow would find it no small matter to bring Mao under control, if for no other reason than that he had been "entrenched in power in Yenan for nearly ten times the length of time that Tito has."[33] And even if Mao and his colleagues were for the time being entirely loyal to Moscow, nationalist temptations following in the wake of new revolutionary power would likely prove too great. The Soviet Union's primary concern with regard to China was "not how the Chinese Communists can be helped to defeat opposition, to win the civil war, but how to ensure complete and lasting control over them and their collaborators. Still green in the Kremlin's memory is its own inept 1927 venture in open intervention, its impetuous masterminding of an Asiatic revolution from Moscow, only to have the revolution 'betrayed' by an intimate collaborator—Chiang Kai-shek."[34]

In addition to accepting the foregoing analysis, the NSC predicted in October, 1948, that once a communist Chinese government was established, it would face a series of perplexing problems, including lack of administrative techniques and widespread social disorder. Sworn by ideology to collectivize and industrialize their society, the communists would "encounter (at least) the passive drag and sly resistance of Chinese individualism and at a maximum disruptive social revolt." Loans and investments from abroad needed to underwrite communist enterprises also would be scarce, and little could be expected from capital-poor Russia. Most important to the council were the diplomatic possibilities should a new Chinese government reveal itself as subservient to the Kremlin. If so, the NSC was certain that the CCP leadership would experience difficulties from the xenophobic Chinese public at large and from nationalist elements within the party: "It is a nice piece of irony that at precisely the time the Chinese Communist leadership is most likely to wish

33. PPS/39, September 15, 1948, in Nelson (ed.), State Department Policy Planning Staff Papers, II, 412–46.
34. Ibid.

to conceal its ties with Moscow, the Kremlin is most likely to be exacting utmost pressure to bring the Chinese Communists under complete control. The possibilities which such a situation would present us, provided we have regained freedom of action, need scarcely be spelled out." [35]

Though the uncertain situation did not permit definite planning, an outline for American policy toward a new Sino-Soviet coalition was beginning to take shape. The NSC first decided that recognition of the Nationalist government would continue until Chiang's final defeat; afterward, recognition of the communist government would depend on circumstances. Further, the council did not consider the menace posed by a communist China alone to be grave. It was only the possibility of China's becoming an adjunct of Soviet power that was dangerous. To prevent this, the NSC adopted a few guiding principles. First, American ability to influence Chinese politics was limited; powerful indigenous forces were in upheaval, effecting a revolutionary transformation. Second, opposition to these forces would doubtless multiply American problems in China and defeat Washington's aims; but by skillfully playing on Chinese ambitions, resentments, and problems, American influence could be enhanced. Similar difficulties and prospects also obtained for Soviet diplomacy in China.

The council concluded that so long as civil war raged, the United States should avoid commitments, military or political, to any particular side: "We must place no reliance on the subjective attitude of any Chinese faction or government toward the U.S. Fear and favor always have and still do control fundamentally the attitude of foreign governments toward us." After the civil war, the United States could favorably dispose of its economic might in the battle for the mind of China. A warning was attached, though: "Economic favor becomes tribute if it continues to be given without expectations. While we must have favors in hand, in the shape of economic authorizations, for the post-Chiang situation, they must not be precommitted. The executive must have the flexibility to give or withhold fully or in part." [36]

By autumn 1948, then, the defeat of Chiang was a foregone conclusion among high-ranking American policy makers. The administration had also accepted some propositions for dealing with post–civil war—regrettably, communist—China. George Kennan feared, however, that the executive flexibility generally recognized as essential to American purposes was in danger, under political and popular assault. Articulate, insistent critics, such as

35. NSC 34, October 13, 1948, NSC File, Modern Military Branch, NA.
36. *Ibid.*

Representative Walter Judd and Senators William Knowland and Pat Mc-
Carren, were impatient of the administration's alleged callousness toward a
once-honored wartime ally. Kennan wrote to Secretary Marshall in late November, "Of major importance at present in the problem of our China policy
are the confusion and bewilderment in the public mind regarding our China
policy. It is important to . . . regain the understanding confidence of the
American public, without which we cannot effectively implement China policy."[37]

Kennan suggested that popular confidence could be restored if Truman employed his office to explain both the nature and course of difficulties encountered in China; such an explanation would ideally emphasize both American
generosity and the ultimate responsibility of the Chinese to determine their
own fate. He also urged the State Department to compile pertinent official
records on Sino-U.S. relations that would enable the government to justify
publicly and in a consistent, persuasive manner American policy toward China.
This last recommendation was not accepted because Marshall and Truman
believed that such a statement would soon prove fatal to Chiang's government. Not until the following spring, when widespread Republican cries
against the administration reached a crescendo, was Kennan's advice taken—
resulting in the controversial *White Paper on China*, issued August 5, 1949.

By the beginning of 1949, three decidedly different attitudes toward China
were evident in the American government. The dominant view in the administration and State Department stressed disengaging from the Nationalists as
gracefully as possible, thereby preserving a position from which to cultivate
influence among the new Chinese rulers. The administration continued aid to
Chiang, primarily to stall communist victory and appease domestic critics unwilling to admit China as a lost cause; however, it vigorously opposed direct
American intervention on grounds that it would confirm the CCP's Marxist-
nationalist suspicion of the West, and popular Chinese support would accrue
to the communists as champions against imperial trespassers.

Although sharing the administration's concern about a costly, unlimited
commitment to Chiang, the Defense Department was willing to risk somewhat more generous measures on his behalf. Admiral William Leahy, ex-
pressing the judgment of the Joint Chiefs of Staff (JCS), recommended in Au-

37. PPS 45, November, 1948, in Nelson (ed.), *State Department Policy Planning Staff Papers*, II, 509–17.

gust, 1948, increased aid and military support to Chiang, if only to delay the time until a communist China could be established and organized.

Finally, some members of Congress—Judd, Knowland, and McCarren, for example—advocated direct intervention, though usually in a vague manner. This was a potentially hazardous, expensive operation; and, when pressed, the congressmen invariably retreated from their positions. Yet for largely political reasons they persisted in emphasizing their disenchantment with the administration's policy, blamed it for China's problems, but plainly failed to offer a realistic alternative American strategy.

Meanwhile, during the winter of 1948–1949, the Nationalist cause was struck by a rapid succession of bewildering calamities. Manchuria fell with the loss of 400,000 KMT troops and all of their equipment. In Mukden, an important Manchurian industrial city, Angus Ward and his staff were held incommunicado by local communists and later were charged with espionage; a full year was to elapse before their release. The Hwai-Hai battle in East China also began badly for the government. And inflation completely slipped out of Chiang's control. The budget deficit was running at the rate of $50 million a month, and public confidence in the government and its currency declined with each military defeat.[38]

38. Tsou, *America's Failure*, 485.

Chapter II

U.S. POLICY TOWARD THE CHINESE COMMUNISTS AND THE SOVIET UNION, 1949

Chiang's position continued to fail in January. Symptomatic of this deteri-orating situation was his removal of more than $300 million of gold bullion to Taiwan and so-called retirement on the twenty-first in favor of General Li Tsung-jen. The generalissimo's "retirement" was a handy fiction that en-abled him to place the burden of defeat on someone else and yet retain all real power among the Chinese Republicans.[1]

Coincidentally, the same day as Chiang's formal abdication, Dean Ache-son was sworn in as secretary of state. His difficult charges were to include effecting American withdrawal from Chiang and keeping China separated from the Soviet Union. The first task was understandably unpleasant. The second was equally complicated and also demanded considerable skill and popular trust. Perhaps a man of great public stature such as George Marshall could have commanded sufficient prestige to cut American ties with Chiang com-pletely and cleanly, though as events later demonstrated, Marshall himself was not immune to attacks from the McCarthy wing of the Republican party. But Acheson proved to be an especially tempting target; he seemed to em-body everything most despised by his critics, who recoiled at his cultivated elegance and privileged background—Groton, Yale, Harvard Law School, partnership in a prominent Washington law firm. How could he, with his British affectations and cosmopolitan tastes, presume to understand either Americans or the nature of their interests abroad? And besides, what were his

1. For an excellent discussion, see Nancy Tucker, "Nationalist China's Decline," in Borg and Heinrichs (eds.), *Uncertain Years*, 131–71.

true allegiances? Many of his opponents feared that this patrician liberal might be too clever, both for his own good and for that of the country. Some were even determined to unmask Acheson as a traitor. They never managed to drive him from office, though not for want of trying, but eventually his critics so damaged public confidence in him that Walter Lippmann sadly advised him to resign, lest paralysis strike down the entire operation of the State Department. Yet Acheson proved to be not only intelligent but also proud and sturdy enough to stand, with Truman's unstinting support, against those enemies arrayed before him. Forebodings of melancholy trials to come were evident even in early 1949.

At his confirmation hearings in mid-January, Acheson, like Marshall before him, attributed Chiang's disasters to incompetent leadership and a disaffected population, not to inadequate American military supplies. Senator Alexander Smith, though, disagreed with the secretary-designate; Smith traced Chiang's problems to Yalta and implied that he had been deliberately betrayed by President Roosevelt. The hearings, both closed and public, were subsequently to reveal an extreme anticommunist congressional posturing that in succeeding months severely handicapped Acheson's policy. Whereas in the meetings he stressed exploiting nationalism in Czechoslovakia, Poland, and Yugoslavia as a means of weakening Soviet power, the senators continually prodded him for an unequivocal anticommunist statement acceptable to the press. Although Acheson considered such witness beside the point, at Senator Arthur Vandenberg's insistence he was finally obliged to equate communism with totalitarianism and to condemn both as fatal to all free peoples. Only Senator Claude Pepper complained about the forced admission: "I am afraid we are reflecting the very hysteria we talk about other people manifesting."[2] Vandenberg retorted that Acheson's testimony would help lessen popular apprehension about him, linked as he was by many people with Alger Hiss.

The administration's plans for phased disengagement from the Republican Chinese were clearly in for trouble when an associate like Vandenberg urged appeasing prejudiced, ill-informed opinion. Given this dreary spectacle, one can also better understand George Kennan's fretful ruminations at the time about whether to resign from the Foreign Service. He observed dryly that "lofty pronouncements of communist tyranny, peace and democracy" had too little to do with "everyday pragmatic problems and anxiety."[3]

2. *Executive Sessions of the Senate Foreign Relations Committee*, II, 33.
3. Kennan to Acheson, January, 1949, Box 64, Acheson Papers.

Respecting China, many press and radio commentators in January endorsed the administration's basic "hands-off" approach, although they lamented communist victories and were fearful of the consequences for American policy should Chiang lose. Some predicted that Mao would become a "Chinese Tito" and that the Soviets might possibly become bogged down in China. The *Magazine of Wall Street* advocated doing business with a communist Chinese government, or a communist-headed coalition, as a means of turning it away from Moscow. An adamant minority, however, including Walter Winchell and William Bullitt, claimed that China could still be "saved" by swift military intervention and aid. And *Life* and the *New York Times* recommended that in the event of a communist triumph, indigenous anti-Mao forces ought to be encouraged and recognition of the new regime withheld.

Already that winter, Anglo-American consultations, initiated by Britain over the problem of recognition, had begun. London's position, conveyed by Ambassador Oliver Franks, was that China's economic deficiencies would hinder future communist consolidation. He advised that new China's desire for diplomatic exchanges and assistance could be shrewdly used as a lever to protect Western political interests and investments.[4] The administration, as we have seen, shared a similar perception but was less confident. Advantages presumed to be gained from early relations between the Chinese communists and Washington conflicted with domestic pressures to save Chiang and with strategic considerations.

American military leaders believed that the predicted communist victory in China posed a menace to Western interests in Taiwan. Since at least 1948, the island had been regarded as an important feature of American Pacific security arrangements. JCS Chief Admiral Leahy had characterized Taiwan as a wartime base useful for the staging of troops and strategic air operations and deemed it vital for control of adjacent shipping routes. In 1949 he urged that the island must be denied to the Soviet Union or a Soviet-dominated China; otherwise, America's adversary could easily dominate "to his advantage and our disadvantage the sea routes between Japan and the Malay area, together with a greatly improved enemy capability of extending his control to the Ryukyus and the Philippines, either of which would produce strategic consequences very detrimental to our national security."[5] The admiral added for good measure that Taiwan's retention was important because it was a poten-

4. *FRUS, 1949*, IX, 5.
5. *Ibid.*, 262.

tial food supplier to Japan, which would soon likely be denied sources in China. General Douglas MacArthur, military governor of Japan, agreed with Leahy's analysis and eventually—in May, 1950—termed the island an unsinkable aircraft carrier, ideal for strikes against the Soviet Far East.

At a time, then, of uninterrupted Nationalist defeats and related problems, including mass desertions and mutiny among army ranks, the JCS and MacArthur affirmed Taiwan's significance. In early February of 1949, they developed plans to establish a modest naval mission on the island; they also sought to subdue CCP agitators and to reassure the native population, itself increasingly restive as Nationalist Chinese swarmed onto Taiwan. The JCS hoped that a small military presence could help stabilize the island while avoiding direct American use of force there.[6] Although the proposal was rejected by the administration, Leahy and MacArthur remained committed to Taiwan as a military base—after some qualms, to be reviewed later—and by promoting it they ultimately championed Chiang.

The National Security Council shared the concern of the JCS about the desirability of preventing communist domination of Taiwan.[7] In early March, the NSC directed that the number of State Department personnel on the island be increased and that an officer of high rank be included. Economic aid under Economic Cooperation Administration (ECA) auspices was also enlarged. This expansion of American activities on Taiwan was officially minimized, however, lest the United States appear to be engaged in civil war–connected actions. National Security Council documents from the period also reveal that the administration was not especially solicitous of Chiang's welfare. Although his buildup on the island was naturally understood as enhancing his position in Taipei's politics, commitments to him did not follow axiomatically. Indeed, on Taiwan itself State Department officials explored opportunities for discreetly aiding Taiwanese independence groups and actively discouraged Chinese immigration. The Americans sought a non-communist-controlled island and were prepared to cooperate with *any* compatible government; a non-Chinese Taiwanese government was considered most preferable.

The Joint Military Advisory Group was withdrawn from China proper in late January, and the American instruction of Nationalist troops ceased. In early February, the NSC also recommended a halt in further aid to mainland

6. *Ibid.*, 286.
7. NSC 37, December 1, 1948; NSC 37/1, January 19, 1949, NSC File, Modern Military Branch, NA.

China, except for a few select shipments, rather than risk new supplies falling into eager communist hands; Generals David Barr and Albert Wedemeyer warned that the "Chinese communists would welcome [assistance] action on our part and wait until the aid arrived and then take it over together with the area."[8] Meanwhile, on the strength of recommendations from the NSC and Kennan, Truman prepared to inform congressional leaders that security considerations would force him in the future to veto any new assistance authorized under the military aid program for China.

An informed optimist in early 1949 could have reasonably concluded that American possibilities for establishing working relations with a Marxist Chinese government were good. According to Mr. Chakravarty, an Indian diplomat in contact with Moscow's ambassador to China, the Soviet government did not relish the notion of pouring scarce supplies and equipment into a vast, impoverished Chinese communist state. Chakravarty also reported that the Soviets feared a Maoist China would develop independent proclivities, like Yugoslavia, and eventually the Soviets would have to garrison large numbers of troops in Siberia to secure Russia's southeastern frontier.[9] From China itself, Clubb and Ambassador Leighton Stuart reported that the Soviets were increasingly unhappy about prospects of CCP victory and were suspicious of an integrated China, whether unified by communists or not.[10] For the moment, the Soviets seemed intent to exploit Chinese natural resources and to establish for Moscow spheres of influence in the northwestern areas. Stuart asserted in late February that Moscow's attempts to secure mining (tungsten and oil), trade, and aviation rights in Sinkiang from the Nationalist regime greatly troubled CCP leaders. "The very existence," he reported, "of Soviet demands on China at a time when the Chinese communists are rapidly gaining the ascendancy seems to indicate something less than comradely trust between the Chinese communists and Moscow and to confirm the hypothesis of a basic conflict between Chinese and Soviet interests."[11] Moreover, the State Department had evidence that Mao was under mounting Soviet pressure to subordinate himself directly to Moscow; the Policy Planning Staff speculated that he was already infected with the "Tito virus."

Late in February, 1949, the National Security Council again reviewed American policy options in China and adopted a number of premises and

8. *FRUS, 1949*, IX, 491.
9. *Ibid.*, VIII, 24–25.
10. Clubb to secretary of state, January 27, 1949, #893/1-2749, RG 59, NA.
11. Memorandum from Ambassador Stuart to Policy Planning Staff, February 25, 1949, #761.93/2-2549, RG 59, NA.

measures suggested by the Policy Planning Staff. First, communist forces were recognized as preponderant everywhere; in due time they would glide across the Yangtze and smash all Nationalist resistance. Only a remnant of the Nationalist government might survive in South China or Taiwan for an uncertain duration of months or perhaps even years. The council also reconfirmed its belief that the Chinese communist leadership, once in power, would confront a myriad of economic difficulties susceptible to American diplomacy. Finally and most important, Chinese communist relations with Russia were held to be fraught with potential baneful problems. The NSC observed, "The full force of nationalism remains to be released in Communist China"; and the inevitable effect of Chinese nationalism would be discord between Peking and Moscow as the Kremlin continued to seek extraterritorial privileges for itself in Manchuria and Sinkiang.

The dispatch of the Soviet ambassador to the Nationalist Foreign Office in Canton, last bastion of the retreating Republican army, indicated to the NSC the depth of Soviet cupidity. As long as Chiang's government controlled or claimed to control any part of the mainland, the Soviets were anxious to strike new territorial deals at China's expense. Soviet negotiations with the Nationalists for special advantages in Sinkiang were, in the words of the NSC, "tidily serving up that province for the USSR no matter who wins out anywhere in China—and are a salutory check on inflated Chinese Communist ambitions." As for the southward move of the Russian ambassador, it seemed to be "an elaborate masquerade of correct Soviet intentions toward the Nationalist Government, warning Mao that the Kremlin had feet in both camps and could do business in a number of directions at once."[12]

Despite ambiguous relations between the Soviets and Chinese communists, the NSC assumed that Mao would remain hostile to the United States for an indeterminate time. American military assistance to the mainland Nationalists, meanwhile, was understood as pathetically ineffective and as contributing ultimately to PLA military strength. Aid to Chiang also helped solidify popular support for the communists, and, worst of all, perpetuated the "delusion" that China's interests lay with the Russians.

The council reckoned that over the next few years, an indigenous Chinese anticommunist "grassroots movement" might emerge that, backed by American support, could displace the uncongenial regime with one friendlier to the West. Consequently, the decision was taken to provide limited assistance

12. *FRUS, 1949*, VIII, 17–18; PPS 49, February 10, 1949, in Nelson (ed.), *State Department Policy Planning Staff Papers*, III, 14–24.

during the post-Chiang period for noncommunist forces resisting Mao. This cautious, problematic program—it remained a part of American diplomatic thinking through November, 1953—was supplemented by immediate practical measures. The NSC decided that the government would continue publicly to affirm both friendship for China and respect for its independence and territorial integrity. The administration would, of course, continue to champion the "Open Door" and recognize the Nationalist government for however long it survived. Yet the administration sought to maintain and cultivate active official contact with all elements in China. Varied contacts, especially with communists, would enable the United States, "while scrupulously avoiding the appearance of intervention, to be alert to exploit through political and economic means, any rifts between the Chinese communists and the USSR and between the Stalinist and other elements in China both within and outside of the communist structure." [13]

According to Acheson's April progress report, consular officers in communist-occupied Peking and Tientsin did stay in constant touch with local party officials. They allowed, among other things, for American information programs to operate undisturbed. Referring to these programs, Acheson recorded that every effort was being made to emphasize the USSR's imperialistic aims in Manchuria, Sinkiang, and Inner Mongolia and to exploit mutual Chinese communist–Soviet suspicions. He added that the implementation of trade policy toward communist areas should provide further means for exploiting rifts between the Chinese Marxists and the USSR. [14]

The NSC posited in its late February deliberations that "in the field of economic relations with China the United States has available its most effective weapons vis-à-vis a Chinese communist regime." These weapons were judged especially impressive if wielded as threats rather than used. Only failing all else should economic intimidation or pressure be concentrated against the Chinese communists; the NSC feared that unbridled economic warfare would drive the Chinese into complete subservience to the USSR. By restoring and maintaining regular economic relations with China, the United States could encourage those party nationalists opposed to exclusive reliance on the Soviet Union. Predicted Chinese resentment of Soviet economic exploitation, occurring while the CCP was hurriedly refurbishing and modernizing the economy, combined with Western trade with China, "might bring about serious conflicts between Kremlin and Chinese communist policy, and thereby tend

13. NSC 34/2, February 28, 1949, NSC File, Modern Military Branch, NA.
14. Acheson, progress report on implementation of NSC 34/2, April 5, 1949, *ibid.*

to produce an independent Chinese communist regime.'' [15] Even if unaccompanied by immediate "positive" results, continued trade relations would help the West exploit Sino-Soviet tensions once they arose. If the hoped-for rift should not emerge at all, the NSC hoped that restored trade could still benefit the West. Foodstuffs from China would be secured for Japan, and substantial British and smaller American investments and enterprises on the mainland could function unmolested, at least for a while.

It should be emphasized that the administration—Acheson and Kennan especially—attached considerable importance to the "economic weapon" as a means of intensifying potential CCP-CPSU conflicts. Signs at the time certainly indicated that the CCP felt economically squeezed and sought to revive and diversify the trade of communist-occupied China. [16] Beginning in April, kerosene and motor gasoline provided by the Standard Oil Company of California and the California–Texas Oil Company were sold to Chinese communist buyers. The administration also quietly encouraged a Manchurian soybean and Japanese consumer goods exchange.

The administration's plans, both to distance itself from Chiang and to loosen CCP-CPSU ties, continually encountered snags in Congress. In a February 5 meeting with congressional leaders, Truman managed to convince them of the futility of sending any more military assistance, allotted or not, to China; but they, in turn, advised him that aid shipments could be delayed only through informal action. In other words, they were unwilling to bear the onus for publicly admitting defeat of America's China client. Vandenberg, in fact, made an emotional public statement the same day promoting the line that American power could still be decisive. At the very least, he exhorted, selfless aid would postpone disaster, for "this blood must not be on our hands." [17] As a result of such antics, the $125 million fund for Nationalist arms was never cut, though some aid deliveries were delayed.

Unabashedly partisan figures also interfered with the administration's plans. The eminent Republican leader Robert Taft charged the president and his advisers with not doing enough on behalf of the Nationalist government. And on February 7, fifty-one Republican congressmen demanded appointment of an independent commission to reexamine American policy in China. Later

15. NSC 41, February 28, 1949, NSC File, *ibid.*
16. *FRUS, 1949*, IX, 910–15.
17. Tsou, *America's Failure*, 499.

that month, dissident Democratic Senator Patrick McCarran introduced a bill
assigning Taipei a loan of $1.5 billion.

Luckily for the administration, it managed through strenuous efforts to
thwart the proposed commission and block increased economic aid to China.
Yet a conciliatory nod toward pro-Nationalist congressmen was made. The
1948 Aid Act, scheduled to expire on April 2, was extended at the administration's initiative until the entire remaining sum of $54 million was spent.
This maneuver hardly soothed the disappointed China bloc, and polemics
against the secretary and president grew shriller. In mid-March, Senator
Bridges, supported by McCarran, accused Acheson of "what might be called
sabotage of the valiant attempt of the Chinese Nationalists to keep at least part
of China free." The two senators also called for a congressional investigation
of the State Department's China policy. Fortunately, these violent attacks received neither much congressional nor popular support. Most news commentators—except the Scripps-Howard Press, Patrick Hurley, and the like—also
still advocated watchful waiting until "the dust settles in China." Respecting
McCarran's proposed large loan, many journalists doubted that any Chinese
leader could use so much money either wisely or effectively for American
ends.[18]

Despite these political victories, the administration's domestic enemies did
not relent, and nasty little skirmishes seemed to flare constantly. One colorful
encounter occurred before a closed session in March of the Senate Committee
on Foreign Relations. Acheson predicted in testimony that Sino-Soviet relations would be intimate immediately following Mao's victory. But he also
professed to see the eventual emergence of Chinese Titoism. Later, com-
menting to Acheson on State Department reorganization plans aimed at increasing central authority, Senator Vandenberg lightheartedly quipped, "This
makes you the Vishinsky of the State Department; is that it?" Adopting a
similar mood, Acheson replied, "I should hope it made me something more
than that." To this Senator Alexander Smith snidely piped, "You do not have
to take orders from the Kremlin in other words." Rankled, Acheson managed
his temper and answered coolly, given the provocation, that his masters were
not in Russia.[19] Ungracious, gratuitous remarks like Smith's were becoming
increasingly commonplace among administration foes; for the first time since
the early 1860s, the loyalty of top-ranking officials was widely impugned

18. *Monthly Survey of American Opinion on International Affairs*, "March, 1949," Division of Public Affairs, Department of State, NA.
19. *Executive Sessions of the Senate Foreign Relations Committee*, II, 96.

without hesitation. Simultaneously, disasters abroad, namely in Asia, lent greater authority to Acheson's local political enemies.

Spectacular communist victories in April, beginning with the Yangtze crossing and capture of Nanking, illustrated anew the Kuomintang's utterly hopeless position and left most of Chiang's army numb, unable to coordinate a serious counteroffensive. Taiwan also seemed helpless against the advancing PLA, and American military chiefs began to doubt the practicality of trying to save the island. In April, Secretary of Defense Louis Johnson reported that the JCS, having considered the critical disparity between American strength and global obligations, opposed military action to prevent a communist-dominated Taiwan. MacArthur also reversed himself completely from previous statements and exclaimed, "There is no earthly military reason why we should need Formosa as a base. It would be of no earthly use to us against our only possible major enemy and certainly they could not utilize it against us." [20] The temporary chief of the ECA China Mission, Allen Griffin, protested against further aid to Taiwan and condemned the Nationalist leaders there for the same corruption that helped lead to defeats on the mainland. He also reviled them for their brutal mistreatment of native Taiwanese.

Amid the onslaught of devastating military defeats and harsh criticisms, President Li and Ambassador Stuart appealed for increased American aid. Stung by criticisms of his regime, Li also wrote a personal letter to Truman in which he apologized for past mistakes and promised reforms and redoubled efforts against the People's Liberation Army. Yet without some Nationalist victory, requests for additional military aid had virtually no chance for approval by Truman or Acheson.

Concomitant with PLA victories, sparking the Pentagon's uncertainty about Taiwan, there was a marked increase in vitriolic anti-American CCP propaganda. Some analysts believed the extreme denunciations proved that Mao and his colleagues were inspired by Moscow and obediently followed it in verbally thrashing the planned North Atlantic pact and America's Asian "imperialism." A more interesting hypothesis, though, and one that reflects greater acumen, was presented by the first-rate American consul in Shanghai, John Cabot. He noted that throughout the world and especially in the United States there had been much public speculation about whether the Chinese communists would drift away from Moscow in a manner similar to the Yugoslavs. It was also clear that Mao had not always faithfully followed Moscow's or-

20. *FRUS, 1949*, IX, 317.

ders. Therefore, figured Cabot, Mao and other CCP leaders must have doubted that the Kremlin had full confidence in them. He wrote, "Lip service is the cheapest kind of service to give Soviet Russia to reassure the latter of the loyalty of the Chinese Communists." He also thought the notable vehemence in CCP anti-American propaganda stemmed from a desire to placate Moscow rather than from any increased hostility to the United States. "If it is assumed that some, but not all, Chinese Communist leaders take orders from Moscow, the same line of thought suggests that those not subservient to Moscow might for reasons of prudence and harmony, go along" with those who followed the party line dictated by the USSR. He went on to stress that the United States should recognize that some CCP leaders "mouthed Soviet propaganda 'with tongue in cheek' in order to conceal their real intention, namely becoming their own masters in China."[21]

In late April, Consul General Clubb advised Acheson along similar lines and added that economic problems in Manchuria and North China were aggravating Soviet anxiety about Chinese aid requirements. Convinced that Soviet apprehensions and hesitation presented an opportunity for inserting a wedge between communist-controlled China and Russia, Clubb recommended promptly increasing trade with PLA-occupied areas.[22]

Prospects of American trade with Communist China were becoming increasingly dim, however. Provocative CCP policies and persistent critics in the United States combined, in effect, against the administration's plans. In the spring, the communists, contrary to normal practice, revoked the legal status of American (and all other Western) consulates and treated their employees merely as private citizens without diplomatic privilege. In connection with Mao's program to eliminate every imperialist vestige, foreign-owned enterprises were also confiscated. Simultaneously, many American analysts and journalists reported a "hate-America" campaign in China. Disturbed and dismayed, public leaders such as Senators Bridges and Knowland and General Claire Chennault issued continuous appeals for generous aid to the Nationalists to rescue as much of the mainland as possible.

The administration for the most part withstood China bloc pressures. A May, 1949, Gallup Poll indicated that the administration still enjoyed popular support for its China policy. The poll revealed that 47 percent of registered voters favored leaving China alone while only 22 percent advocated "saving" the Nationalists. Washington did agree to mint silver coins for the republic at cost,

21. John Cabot to Ambassador Stuart, April 20, 1949, #893.00B/4-2049, RG 59, NA.
22. *FRUS, 1949*, IX, 976.

but the action was insufficient to slow down the exponential rise of Chinese inflation. Republican China's economic woes were not seriously mitigated, and its armies continued to reel before unforgiving blows.

In May the PLA, meeting little resistance, traversed nearly two hundred miles beyond the Yangtze and surrounded Shanghai. Beginning with this period, CCP representatives made their first overtures toward the West and the United States in particular. Apparently, although this cannot be absolutely confirmed, these moves were discreetly undertaken by pragmatic leaders of the party such as Chou En-lai, who were anxious to check Li Li-san, Kao Kang, and insidious Soviet influence.

Ambassador Stuart telegraphed Washington in early May that the "Chinese Communists have lost no opportunities in emphasizing lack of recognition and official relationship between USA and themselves."[23] And yet, as soon became evident, not just any price for recognition was acceptable to the communists, especially if payment jeopardized recent achievements won by prolonged, arduous struggle. To emphasize the point, CCP representative Huang Hua told the ambassador that it would be up to Washington when the appropriate time arrived to make the first move in establishing relations with the People's Democratic Government; at the same time, however, Huang displayed a lively interest in American recognition of Communist China on terms of equality and mutual benefit.[24] Later that month, Chou En-lai, acting cautiously through a "reliable intermediary" (his name is not known even now), tried to signal local American government representatives. According to Clubb, Chou claimed that the Soviet Union could not possibly provide the vast amounts of aid required by China; only the United States and Great Britain could realistically afford to help the CCP rebuild and modernize the country. Chou apparently favored normal relations with the United States, which he hoped would be forthcoming with assistance to China, as in the past. Clubb also reported that Chou's "liberal" faction was locked in a struggle with party radicals and that a critical issue between them was whether to rely exclusively on the Soviet Union: "As spokesman for liberal wing he could say that when time came for Communist participation in international affairs his group would work within party for sensible solution [to the] impasse between USSR and West and would do its best [to make] the USSR discard policies leading to

23. Ambassador Stuart to secretary of state, May 3, 1949, #711.93/5-349, RG 59, NA.
24. The Huang-Stuart meetings were moving, sometimes harrowing, and ultimately led nowhere. For a fine assessment see Robert Blum, *Drawing the Line: The Origin of the American Containment Policy in East Asia* (New York, 1982), 53–64.

war.''[25] Chou hoped, therefore, that American officials would recognize that practical, nondoctrinaire elements existed in the CCP and that they wanted to establish regular, working relations between China and the United States as quickly as possible. Clubb was greatly encouraged.

Both Stuart and Acheson expected to exact communist acceptance of "international obligations"—relating to the safety of American citizens and property in China and repayment of large American loans accumulated by the central government—in exchange for recognition. At the very least, the Americans hoped that Mao would formally repudiate his declaration of 1947 in which he proclaimed that the CCP should not honor foreign loans granted to previous Chinese governments. The State Department contended that withholding recognition from the revolutionary regime, which was allegedly anxious for international acceptance, might temper its excessive policies; formal Chinese-American relations would in any event clearly benefit the United States because latent Peking Titoists could have another alternative than the Soviet Union to turn toward.

On June 15, Mao delivered a party speech in which he expressed his regime's desire for normal relations and trade with all countries, including capitalist ones. After demanding that other states sever relations with the Chinese reactionaries, he declared, "The Chinese people wish to have friendly cooperation with the people of all countries and to resume and expand international trade in order to develop production and promote economic prosperity.''[26] Clubb and Stuart believed the speech was in earnest, and they advised Washington that a favorable American response would be well received by the CCP leadership. Unfortunately, the administration was inhibited, unable to provide a decisive reply. In late June, a bipartisan Senate group composed of sixteen Republicans and five Democrats urged Truman not to recognize a Chinese communist government; heavily publicized mistreatment of American citizens and diplomats also contributed to an atmosphere inconducive to recognition. Still, Acheson and Foreign Service officers in China remained confident that fairly soon the CCP would act in a more cooperative, mutually helpful manner.

Consul Clubb advised that American food and economic assistance to stave off a predicted summer famine were urgently needed in China: "It is probably already clear to both Soviet and Chinese Communists that USSR is unable to supply China's economic needs, both may be reconciled to necessity of

25. *FRUS, 1949*, VIII, 357–60.
26. *Selected Writings from the Works of Mao Tse-Tung* (Peking, 1967), iv.

China's having to deal with USA to avoid calamitous economic collapse.''
He recommended, ''For so long as Communist China is run for political benefit [of] USSR let it pay a barrel head for what it receives, either in economic
equivalent or in terms [of] political concessions designed [to] break up its alliance with USSR.'' During Ambassador Stuart's June meetings with Huang,
the latter repeatedly emphasized CCP desires for recognition as the government of China; Stuart posed inflexible, however, and in accordance with standard practice, denied the possibility of recognition until Mao formally established a new government. Behind the ambassador's legal argument lay the
State Department's desire to press for Chinese concessions.[27]

According to the historian Robert Blum, by July the Americans had over-
played their hand. Blum argues that as prospects for early American recognition faded, the CCP's attachment of importance to relations with Washington sharply declined. Official communist pronouncements expressed
unequivocal anger and resentment toward the great ''imperialist power.'' The
Chinese communists blamed the United States for the Nationalist port blockade, bombings of Shanghai and Nanking, and organization of a volunteer air
force for attacks against the mainland. Citing Ambassador Stuart, Blum concludes that the militant anti-Western wing of the CCP was vindicated by
Washington's ineffective response to Chinese overtures. Certainly, the moderate communist position represented by Huang and Chou seemed discredited—to many observers at the time, including Ambassador Stuart, and to
scholars since—when Mao announced on July 1 that China would ''lean to
the side of the Soviet Union.''[28]

In this message, Mao explained that the Chinese communist experience of
twenty-eight years had demonstrated the wisdom of siding with progressive
forces; now all of China had to choose between the camps of imperialism and
socialism. A third way did not exist; a third road was merely an illusion. He
further stated, ''Not only in China but throughout the world, one must lean
either to imperialism or socialism. There is no exception. Neutrality is a cam-
ouflage.'' He went on to detail how the success of any genuine people's revolution depended upon aid from ''international revolutionary forces.'' In the
case of China, ''even when victory is won, it cannot be made without such

27. Edmund Clubb to secretary of state, June 2, 1949, Telegram 928, Truman Papers; Ambassador Stuart to secretary of state, June 8, 1949, #711.93/6-849, RG 59, NA.
28. Robert Blum, *The United States and Communist China in 1949 and 1950* (Washington,
1973).

outside help.'' The imperialist world clearly could not be counted on to assist a people's government.

On the basis of these remarks, Tang Tsou in his authoritative study *America's Failure in China* holds that Mao's speech was ''an historic pronouncement on foreign policy'' and amounted to a complete break with the West: ''Ideological convictions . . . combined with hostility toward the United States [led] Mao to make a sharp break with the age-old Chinese policy of using barbarians to control barbarians.'' [29] Both Tsou and Blum contend that the speech also had a sobering effect on American policy makers and left officials pessimistic about early-developing Chinese Titoism.

Yet another interpretation of Mao's words might be closer to the mark. In the first place, preliberation Soviet-Chinese party relations, as noted in Chapter II, suffered from problems largely connected with Soviet-Comintern interference. During its long struggle, the CCP developed resourcefulness and self-reliance that eventually enabled it to prevail with little Russian aid. Whereas obedience to Soviet orders caused setbacks in 1927, initiative independent of Stalin resulted in the 1949 communist victory. Mao, then, was surely not entirely sincere when he exclaimed that for decades the CCP had received invaluable assistance from the socialist world.

Moreover, his remark about a successful revolution's need for help in safeguarding its security and prosperity was obviously a request, perhaps for Soviet food relief and economic succor, but at the very least for formal recognition. The rhetoric about the nonexistence of any third road was probably meant to allay Stalin's fears of Chinese Titoism, thereby smoothing the flow of needed Soviet assistance. Protestations of loyalty also undoubtedly enhanced the chairman's esteem, at least in the eyes of party ''radicals,'' and perhaps bolstered Mao's immunity to Russian interference; after all, the Soviets might find someone like Kao Kang more worthy or more compliant than Mao to lead the largest nation into communism. As we shall see shortly, Mao had good reason on more than one occasion to wonder how far the Kremlin would go in advancing its own candidate's cause.

Finally, Mao's declaration of solidarity with Russia might have been exacted by Moscow as prepayment on forthcoming Soviet aid. At the time, Soviet prestige certainly needed boosting: the ill-conceived Berlin blockade had just been lifted; an American-inspired security pact, the North Atlantic Treaty Organization (NATO), aimed against Russia was forming; Tito was as yet

29. Tsou, *America's Failure*, 505.

unrepentant; and communist guerrillas in Greece had been pummeled. A demonstration of Chinese friendship for the Soviet Union would partly compensate for various Russian diplomatic embarrassments.

In any case, Mao did not entirely rule out the possibility of continued trade and working relations with the West. Rather, mindful of Soviet fears and party hard-liners, he proceeded cautiously in his July message: "We want to do business. We only oppose domestic and foreign reactionaries who hamper us from doing business. Unite all forces at home and abroad to smash domestic and foreign reactionaries and there will be business, and the possibility of establishing diplomatic relations with all foreign countries on the basis of equality, mutual benefits, and mutual respect for territorial sovereignty."[30]

Briefly put, "leaning to one side" constituted only cautious acceptance of Soviet leadership and limited dependence on Moscow. Mao's remark about mutual respect of territorial sovereignty was surely aimed directly at Russia, the only country then encroaching on Chinese soil. Though the imperialistic United States was admittedly untrustworthy and sided with Mao's civil opponents, new China was nevertheless willing to conduct business and enter into "diplomatic relations with all foreign countries." As an official Chinese interpretation of Mao's message stated shortly afterward, " 'Leaning to one side' is our basic policy and course, but it does not call for the abandonment of proper international strategy."[31] In other words, flexibility informed by economic and diplomatic requirements rather than rigid adherence to principle or unqualified devotion to ideology would characterize Chinese policy.

In response, the administration did not drastically modify its plans to draw China away from the Soviet Union. Mao's words were not taken at face value; some analysts even suspected that they were made under duress. The consul general in Shanghai reported to Acheson that, according to reliable sources, Mao sulked after the speech. These Chinese informants alleged that he had adopted an inflated pro-Soviet line because he feared that otherwise Soviet forces along the border would intervene against him, directly or through agents.[32]

In a memorandum concerning Taiwan's predicted fall, composed only five days after Mao's speech, Kennan did not even mention Soviet advantages related to Mao's talk. He did note, however, "growing restlessness in Chinese

30. *Selected Writings of Mao Tse-Tung,* iv.
31. Simmons, *Strained Alliance,* 64.
32. Consul general in Shanghai to Acheson, August 10, 1949, #76!.93/8-1049, RG 59, NA.

Communist circles over Russian imperialism in Manchuria.''[33] Indeed, throughout July and August, State Department officers were favorably impressed by the prospect of deterioriating CCP-Soviet relations. In late July, a trade delegation led by Kao Kang arrived in Moscow. Representing the so-called Manchurian People's Democratic Authorities, the delegation negotiated commercial treaties with the Kremlin. To most State Department observers the concluding agreements confirmed Soviet designs to detach industrialized Manchuria from China. America's ambassador to the Soviet Union, Alan Kirk, suspected that the Kremlin hoped to establish quasi-independent Chinese socialist republics out of Sinkiang and Inner Mongolia, as well as Manchuria. And if a legitimate CCP-Soviet settlement over Manchuria should eventuate, Kirk doubted that China would benefit much. The USSR would not be able to fulfill its pledges of economic aid, and even if it did, the ''Soviets would exploit fruits thereof for their own purposes and thus reveal to Chinese Communists and 'progressives' the true nature of Soviet imperialism.''[34]

Eager not to involve itself further with activities likely to increase Peking's antagonism, the administration decided in August definitely not to intervene on Taiwan's behalf, even if Chiang's forces were threatened by fatal blows. Kennan, however, was not entirely convinced of the wisdom of surrendering all interests on Taiwan. At one point he actually suggested that American military forces take the island from Chiang, administer its defenses, and establish an ''independent'' government; he argued that the island garrison could thus be effectively protected from invasion and internal decay. This odd proposal, though, never got anywhere. More important, the Joint Chiefs of Staff concurred with the administration's decision in August and rejected any notion that Taiwan was of essential strategic significance. But they prudently

33. *FRUS, 1949*, IX, 357.

34. *Ibid.*, 963. An alternative interpretation suggests that the Manchurian People's Democratic Authorities were a fictional convenience and provided the only form by which Moscow could receive Chinese Communists and still recognize the KMT. Certainly the Soviets were capable of delicate subterfuge and on different occasions succeeded with it. So far, no evidence, apart from State Department speculation, has appeared that either undermines or supports such a hypothesis. Given Kao's predisposition toward Russia, his unmasking in 1954 as a ''foreign agent,'' and the fact that he represented merely one faction in the party, my own hunch is that once securely in power, Mao was anxious to undo Kao's agreement with the Soviets and to repudiate any independent Manchurian political authority. Kao's unhappy relations with Mao are further described in Chapter V.

added that "future circumstances, extending to war itself, might make overt military action with respect to Formosa eventually advisable."[35]

At the time, the East-West propaganda war was already in full swing. During the late summer of 1949, Voice of America and other "informational programs" worked steadily to foster a potential schism between the Chinese communists and the Soviets. These propaganda programs emphasized the imperialistic aim of the USSR in China and attempted to destroy "the fiction that the USSR is the champion and protector of Chinese nationalism."[36]

America's greatest propaganda trump, of course, was its economic might. Pursuant to Acheson's economic policy toward Communist China, designed to hasten its drift away from Russia, the State Department sanctioned the sale of thirteen hundred metric tons of copper wire by two private firms to a North China railway. Limited petroleum exports were also still allowed. Department officials were nonetheless concerned about ongoing unrestricted British exports to China, for London's actions threatened to undermine the West's presumed economic leverage over Communist China. Both the administration and London had previously agreed that the CCP should be made to realize that, without the West, economic problems would persist in afflicting China. Acheson and Kennan had understood that during the final months of civil war, Great Britain and the United States would limit their economic relations with the new government; as noted earlier, they sought specific goals of political and diplomatic reciprocity for expanded trade and American material support. Yet the British decided that investments and financial interests in China and Hong Kong dictated a narrower, more purely economic diplomacy.

On learning of Chinese petroleum imports from the United States, Senator Knowland condemned them, despite State Department assurances that the quantities shipped provided only a fraction of Chinese domestic needs. Incidentally, the Gallup Polls that summer registered widespread support for the senator's stand: 46 percent of the American voters opposed trade with China, 37 percent favored it, and 41 percent were against recognition of a communist regime with 19 percent in favor. Moreover, as the PLA started its final campaigns, the public clamor for action increased. Many prominent citizens, such as Robert Taft and Thomas Dewey, loudly denounced the administration's "losing policy." Kennan observed: "It is apparent that in the

35. NSC 37/7, August 22, 1949, NSC File, Modern Military Branch, NA.
36. NSC progress report on the implementation of NSC 34/2, August 19, 1949, Modern Military Branch, NA.

American public our policy toward Asia is suffering from an acute case of negativism. That the objective situation does not permit a wide range of solid action on our part is not adequately understood and, even if it were, would not satisfy the demand in the American nature for 'positive action.' '' He trusted, however, that the *China White Paper*, scheduled for release in August, would ''go far toward justifying our policy toward China and quiet most of our critics.'' [37]

The fateful decision not to intervene in the Chinese civil war was made partly on the assumption that public opinion would not support a large-scale military operation shortly after the end of World War II and mass demobilization. Still, in response to numerous allegations of acquiescence, sellout, and betrayal, the administration issued its famous China report. Distributed on August 5, the monumental, documented history of Sino-American relations since 1944 explained American attempts to promote a stable, democratic China sympathetic to the United States. The extent of aid granted the Nationalist regime and General Marshall's valiant attempt to mediate peace and form a government representing all political parties, including the communists, were carefully reviewed. The impossibility of imposing a settlement was attributed to the ''distrust of the leaders of both the Nationalist and Communist Parties for each other'' that ''proved too deep to permit final agreement.'' The report asserted further that the civil war's ominous result was beyond the control of the American government: ''Nothing that this country could have done within the reasonable limits of its capabilities could have changed that result; nothing that was left undone by this country could have contributed to it. It was the product of internal forces, forces which this country tried to influence but could not. A decision was arrived at within China, if only a decision by default.'' [38]

According to the secretary of state, Chiang's corrupt, unpopular regime could not withstand the popular-based, ''fanatical'' communists. Acheson neglected to say, of course, that neither could the American government's half-measure policy—providing military aid to Chiang but avoiding troop commitments—possibly contain the seemingly irresistible force of radical nationalism.

The government report was a curious blend of candor—admitting that the

37. Kennan's ''Suggested Course of Action in East and South Asia,'' July 8, 1949, Policy Planning Staff Papers, RG 59, NA.
38. Acheson's ''Letter of Transmittal'' in L.P. Van Slyke (ed.), *The China White Paper* (2 vols., Stanford, 1967), I, xvi.

United States was unable to do much about events in China—and myth. In the "Letter of Transmittal," Acheson dignified the doubtful notion of monolithic international communism directed by Moscow: "The Communist leaders have publicly announced their subservience to a foreign power, Russia, which during the last fifty years has been assiduous in its efforts to extend its control in the Far East." Yet at the same time Acheson intimated the thrust of American policy. He suggested that Sino-Soviet links were fragile and that despite gloomy Far Eastern developments, there was some cause for hope: "Ultimately the profound civilization and the democratic individualism of China will reassert themselves and she will throw off the foreign yoke. I consider that we should encourage all developments in China which now and in the future work toward this end."[39]

One may reasonably wonder what Acheson had in mind in his allusion to China's "democratic individualism." It is, after all, a peculiarly Western notion and has little obvious applicability in a Chinese cultural-historical context. In part, the phrase illustrates the universalism in which American policy was cast during the late 1940s. It may also have been intended to reassure the American public, fearful of totalitarianism triumphant, that communism in China was fundamentally ephemeral. Still, Acheson's statement concerning the need to encourage "the Chinese people" in resisting Soviet domination reflected in part, if not fully, both State Department and administration policy.[40]

Declarations of support to indigenous anticommunist Chinese forces in the *White Paper*, although aimed at the American public, angered the revolution's leaders in Peking. The statements, in retrospect certainly unwise insertions, served to aggravate CCP suspicions about the United States, confirmed ideological interpretation, and revealed Washington's intention to support Chiang. The pronouncements thus inadvertently helped undermine Acheson's cautious policy. As he later told the National Press Club, the United States must "not seize the unenviable position which the Russians have carved out for themselves. We must not undertake from the Russians to ourselves the

39. *Ibid.*, xvii.
40. A number of American journalists and writers tried to popularize the administration's policy premises and make them more explicit. Typical was a pre–Korean War review of the Cold War by Admiral Ellis Zacharias: "Neither do we expect the Chinese to fall blind victims to communism as it is directed from Moscow. But we can expect dissidence to develop and spread and even activate itself in the form of the kind of resistance to the Kremlin that Mao and his men showed to the Kuomintang. Whether we call it Maoism or Chinese nationalism, it is a reality with which we have to deal and upon which we must count in making our plans" (*Behind Closed Doors: The Secret History of the Cold War* [New York, 1950], 113–14).

righteous anger, the wrath and the hatred of the Chinese people which must develop. It would be folly to deflect it to ourselves."[41] But for many observers in Peking, these remarks did not outweigh views expressed by "militarists" in Congress and at the Pentagon. Hard-liners pointed to hostile actions confessed by Acheson himself in the *White Paper*—namely, American aid of anti-Peking resistance. At best, the public discussion suggested conflicting attitudes in Washington, causing temporary indecisiveness in U.S. diplomacy.

The predisposition of most communists obviously was to assume Western antagonism and the worst possible outcome from American policy debate. In the August 15 edition of *Jen-min-jih-pao*, Mao declared that imperialists "make trouble, fail, make trouble again, fail again . . . till their doom; that is the logic of the imperialists and all reactionaries the world over in dealing with the people's cause, and they will never go against this logic. This is a Marxist law. When we say 'imperialism is ferocious,' we mean that its nature will never change, that the imperialists will never lay down their butcher knives, that they will never become Buddhas till their doom." Those party members, including Chou, who had probed American intentions only weeks before, were now in more delicate positions vis-à-vis their comrades. Thanks to Mao, all incorrect attitudes were repudiated, and those who had strayed could be rescued from wrong opinion. Clubb speculated that Chou's earlier orchestrated démarche, which included Huang's conversations with Stuart, precipitated new Soviet attempts in August to increase leverage over the CCP. The *White Paper* revelations played directly into Soviet advantage; for this reason, feared Clubb, Chou and his group were very much on the defensive.[42]

The *White Paper*'s repercussions in China not only strengthened the position of party members who favored closer relations with Moscow but also blunted the influence of noncommunists—potentially not great anyway—on party policy. American Counselor Jones reported from Nanking that references to democratic individualism in the "Letter of Transmittal" had severely weakened the position of third-party, noncommunist elements on the mainland, who had hoped to exert a moderating influence on pro-Soviet and extremist groups within the CCP. He feared that the *White Paper* was being used as a weapon to weaken and neutralize these elements through charges that they were receiving aid from the United States. This situation had forced

41. Blum, *United States and Communist China*, 4.
42. *FRUS, 1949*, VIII, 496–97.

a number of prominent noncommunists to condemn the *White Paper* in public "in order to clear themselves of suspicion."[43]

In the United States, release of the *White Paper* proved profoundly disappointing to Kennan: instead of cooling public passions it both inflamed misunderstanding and spurred wild domestic debate. Normally dispassionate, Walter Lippmann marveled at Chiang's "stranglehold on American policy"; he was also astonished to learn that between the end of World War II and March, 1949, the United States had provided financial aid to China worth roughly $1,986.3 million and military aid valued at $1,000.7 million. William Loeb's reaction was quite different. In an intemperate letter to Truman, Loeb charged, "In an attempt to whitewash State Department failure the *White Paper* stoops to an incomplete, misleading and partly untruthful presentation." Senator Knowland claimed the report proved Chiang was "right and the United States was wrong" about the threat of worldwide communist conspiracy.[44]

Undaunted by Nationalist defeats and *White Paper* criticisms of Chiang and fortified by MacArthur's public proclamation that the PLA was grossly overrated and American intervention could still reverse the battle, Knowland, Walter George, John Vorys, and Walter Judd managed to force administration acceptance in September of a new China aid bill. By threatening to delay or otherwise jeopardize the administration's plans for aid to Europe, the China bloc skillfully negotiated assistance for Republican China, providing up to $75 million in military assistance to the "general area of China." Ultimately, the appropriated funds never reached the Nationalist government; American prestige was not enhanced nor communist victory postponed.

The bill's passage reconfirmed to Peking both America's hostility, already amply documented in the *White Paper*, and continued commitment to Chiang. Mao responded by categorically demanding that the United States abandon the Kuomintang and "designs on Taiwan." Lo Lung-chi, a leader of the Democratic League, also warned the United States and the UN General Assembly against further considerations to the Nationalist government. As far as the State Department could tell, however, neither Lo nor Mao, despite growing impatience, dismissed the possibility of regular Sino-American relations.

43. *Ibid.*, IX, 1407.
44. William Loeb to Truman, August 24, 1949, Truman Papers; *Monthly Survey of American Opinion on International Affairs*, "August, 1949," Division of Public Affairs, Department of State, NA.

Canton's fall and Mao's declaration of a People's Republic of China on October I sharpened debate within the United States and among its allies and others about whether to recognize Peking and grant it a UN seat. India's Jawaharlal Nehru urged immediate Western recognition. The British, although not indifferent to the diplomatic advantages of withholding accreditation for awhile, still felt constrained both by large investments in China and by Hong Kong's vulnerability to PLA attack. In the United States, most prominent commentators expected *de facto* American recognition fairly soon, though a number of public opinion polls indicated that the majority of citizens still opposed official recognition.

Acheson believed that for formal, full Sino-American relations to be palatable to his compatriots, a show of good faith by China was required. In other words, he needed a sharp, snappy demonstration of Chinese moderation and reasonableness. Soon after the establishment of Mao's government, the secretary specified that certain conditions would have to be met before American recognition was extended. He declared that the new rulers had to prove that they controlled the territory of China, that they governed by consent of their subjects, and that they responsibly accepted all "international obligations." Although he expressed himself in a measured manner acceptable to congressional and popular opinion, Acheson did try to indicate that the administration was genuinely interested in relations with new China.

Some American diplomats posted abroad, notably Ambassador Kirk and Consul General Clubb, objected to the secretary's slow, deliberate recognition policy and worried that the United States was dissipating its political and economic assets. In October, Kirk sent a message to his superiors in which he emphasized the *immediate* advantages of early recognition: the government needed on-the-spot reporting, was obliged to protect American citizens and property in China, and would benefit greatly by the inevitable influence and contact between embassy officers and communist personnel. He reminded the secretary that the embassy staff would occupy an excellent position from which to disseminate Western views and exploit to American advantage Soviet imperialism in Manchuria, China, and elsewhere.[45]

Clubb argued in a similar vein and stressed quick deployment of economic weapons; the Chinese communists should realize as soon as possible that concrete benefits could "be obtained through commerce and good relations with non-Soviet countries." It had to be impressed upon CCP leaders, he contin-

45. *FRUS, 1949*, IX, 107.

ued, that political and economic relations with the West, and with America in particular, promised more profit to China than exclusive dependence on Russia. He also reported that in recent weeks few anti-American stories had been published by the Chinese press, a good sign, presumably, that Peking was serious about Sino-American cooperation. Incidentally, all partici-pants—academics, prominent businessmen, and lawyers—at the State De-partment's October Round Table Conference (except for Harold Stassen and one or two others) favored early recognition of China. In Peking, meanwhile, the future of Sino-American cooperation was also receiving close attention.[46]

To Mao, fulfillment of "international obligations," which included re-spect for precommunist treaties and guaranteed protection of American en-terprises in China, smacked of traditions contrary to the new socialist order. The American conditions, once known, were rejected. Chinese displeasure was evident in new incidents that involved sometimes brutal mistreatment of American diplomats and reckless disregard for American-owned property. Episodes embarrassing to the United States culminated in communist seizure of part of the American diplomatic compound on January 14, 1950, and led directly to withdrawal of all American officials from China.

Departing from American wishes, the British took measures in early Oc-tober to assure friendly and mutually advantageous relations, both commercial and political, with the new regime. Informal contacts were immediately es-tablished between British consular officers and Chinese communist authori-ties. Administration officials were much disappointed by the breach in their united-front approach to Chinese recognition; and yet, aware of British con-cerns behind the action, Truman was unwilling to take measures that might relieve Whitehall's underlying fears. In fact, the National Security Council decided in October that the "United States will not provide military support to the British for the defense of Hong Kong in the event of Communist mil-itary attack, under present circumstances or presently foreseeable circum-stances."[47] Consequently, the British felt they lacked any alternative but to reach some accommodation, no matter how shabby it might seem to Wash-ington, with the revolutionaries or else stand by helpless as their possessions and colony were repossessed. In early January, 1950, Great Britain led a number of noncommunist European states, including the Netherlands, Switz-erland, and the Scandinavian countries, in recognizing the People's Repub-lic. India prepared to establish relations with China, and Nehru again urged

46. *Ibid.*, 114.
47. NSC 55/2, October 17, 1949, NSC File, Modern Military Branch, NA.

the Americans to do the same. He stressed the revolution's importance to Asians, delighted that one of their own had defied the white, imperial world order. Only the French were steadfast in cleaving to the American line. Indochina High Commissioner Léon Pignon, for one, feared that conferring legitimacy on Mao's regime would encourage Ho's Vietminh insurgents.

Late in October of 1949, and again acting carefully through agents, Chou tried to reach American officials in the hope of salvaging Peking-Washington relations. While he reportedly said that the Americans were dreaming if they really expected the CCP to split away from Russia, he insisted that the Chinese Marxists would not always be anti-American: "The . . . Party cannot afford two enemies at one time, but there is nothing to keep [it] from having more than one friend." According to American intelligence, Chou was unfortunately unable to push very hard among his colleagues for better relations with Washington. He was both restrained by a powerful pro-Moscow CCP faction and unwilling to risk losing Soviet friendship by making insistent overtures to America.[48]

Despite some misgivings over the possible deleterious effect on policy of not recognizing Peking, the administration remained convinced through December that Sino-Soviet problems were brewing and would rebound to American advantage. In mid-October, Acheson's trusted adviser Philip Jessup was queried by senators anxious to know if the Chinese communists might "pull an à la Tito." Jessup explained, "We think there is a real possibility that the evolution of the situation of China vis-à-vis the Soviet Union, the attempt which the Soviet Union will probably make to exercise greater control on the Chinese . . . may bring about the same kind of antagonism between the Chinese Communists and the Russians, which would develop a Tito movement."[49]

Through different news agencies Washington's concern for the Chinese people's independence and welfare was repeatedly broadcast to the mainland. The principal objective of the propaganda—much of it actually covert and attributable to non-American sources—was, of course, the "exposure of Soviet imperialism."[50] Moreover, firms conducting business in China were allowed to continue their operations, as were philanthropic and educational missions. Export of strategic items was increasingly restricted, though, lest

48. Admiral Hillenkoetter, memorandum, November, 1949, *Declassified Documents Quarterly*, III (October–December, 1977), 261.

49. Blum, *United States and Communist China*, 4.

50. "US Propaganda to China: Allocation of Responsibilities Between Overt and Covert Operations," November 7, 1949, unnumbered PPS document, RG 59, NA.

they wind up in Soviet or North Korean hands; petroleum deliveries were also steadily reduced to ever smaller fractions of minimal civilian consumption needs. By this policy, mixing economic inducement and implied threat, Acheson hoped to demonstrate the United States's importance for China.

The administration's policy of coaxing the CCP away from Russia continued to meet domestic political obstacles and resistance from CCP "extremists." In late October, Consul General Ward and four members of his staff in Mukden, who had previously been held incommunicado, were jailed by local Chinese authorities. The Hearst and Scripps-Howard newspapers, Senators Knowland and Bridges, and Representatives Judd, Joseph Martin, and Robert Wagner demanded rescue and raged against "spineless" Democratic leaders who balked before resolute action.[51] For a brief period, Truman did seriously consider imposing a naval blockade against China as a means to force release of the hostages. Acheson, however, insisted on treating the matter with extreme delicacy and warned that the United States should not take any steps that might dignify or legitimize the extraordinary behavior of the "pro-Moscow" Mukden communists. On December 12, the American diplomats were freed after a trial in which they were found guilty of spying. By convening the trial, the local authorities tried to justify their own illegal behavior and were able to make propaganda points against America. By their subsequent "magnanimous" gesture—or perhaps at the behest of higher officials elsewhere—they also demonstrated that future relations with the United States were possible, even desirable.

The last major domestic-based challenge to administration policy in 1949 came in late December, when the Pentagon once again revised its estimates of Taiwan's military importance. Under the signature of JCS Chairman General Omar Bradley, the Pentagon chiefs submitted a recommendation for military aid, including stationing American soldiers, and substantial political-economic support of Taipei. Through these programs the island could be buttressed and integrated into "the overall program of resisting the spread of Communist domination in East Asia."[52] The Joint Chiefs' proposal precipitated a furor with the State Department.

On December 29, Secretary Acheson met at the Pentagon with Generals Bradley, Joseph Collins, and Lauris Norstad and Admiral Forrest Sherman to clarify and resolve questions. Acheson opened the discussion by stating that

51. *Monthly Survey of American Opinion on International Affairs*, "November 1949," Division of Public Affairs, Department of State, NA.
52. *FRUS, 1949*, IX, 460–61.

he understood from previous JCS estimates that Taiwan's strategic significance was minor and did not warrant employment of American armed forces.
Besides, he pointed out, the JCS well knew that the NSC did not expect Taiwan to withstand internal decline, communist subversion, or reintegration with
the mainland for much longer. Given this understanding, the secretary professed puzzlement with the JCS stand and regarded it as a shift from previous
positions. Thereupon, Bradley objected and claimed that the Joint Chiefs had
always been consistent; they had traditionally maintained that the island was
valuable but had not pressed eagerly for retaining it because sufficient funds
for such a task had been unavailable until recently. On October 6, when the
Military Assistance Act was approved, ample monies had been released to
support the preferred policy. He also argued that the transfer from the mainland to Taiwan of Nationalist air force units, ships, and ground forces had
substantially increased the island's worth. Taiwan's need for imported gasoline, bombs, ammunition, and maintenance parts had grown proportion-
ately. General Collins explained further that, based on October intelligence
reports, relatively small American expenditures could help Taiwan survive
for a longer time than originally thought possible. He asserted that a protracted Chinese campaign against Taiwan would not only delay communist
consolidation but would also divert Peking, at least temporarily, from moves
against Indochina, Burma, and Siam.

Acheson, patient but unconvinced, responded with a well-constructed review of the department's Far Eastern analysis and its bearing on Taiwan. First,
he dismissed a communist invasion of Southeast Asia as altogether unlikely;
instead, local communists would probably rely on sabotage and exploitation
of internal problems. As a counter, the United States should align itself with
non-Marxist nationalist movements and aid them in establishing stability, improving the standard of living, and increasing food production. Respecting
the Chinese communists and their Soviet ally, Acheson pleaded the long view
and argued that in the Soviet effort to detach the northern provinces of China
lay the seeds of future conflict between the two countries. Mao, moreover,
was "not a true satellite in that he came to power by his own efforts and was
not installed in office by the Soviet Army." This set of circumstances
amounted to an important asset in the Far East, and "it would have to be for
a very important strategic purpose that we would take an action which would
substitute ourselves for the Soviets as the imperialist menace to China."[53]

53. *Ibid.*, 466.

For these reasons, explained Acheson, the department opposed waging economic warfare against Communist China and was determined that the United States not take any actions that might play into the hands of CCP hardliners and Moscow henchmen. Although the United States was not about to sanction the sale of strategic materials to China, neither should it provide any basis for propaganda that American actions were responsible for the inevitable economic problems that China would encounter while under communist rule. In fact, China and Japan, natural trade partners, should be encouraged to revive economic relations.

The position of the United States in China resembled that of the Soviet Union in 1927, "when she was driven from China and her influence liquidated. It has taken her twenty-two years to return to a position of influence and it may similarly take us as long . . . it is against this backdrop that the Department of State looks at Formosa." He further explained that the island was not in danger of falling to invasion but that internal decay would probably cause it to collapse: "With a hostile population, overrun by refugees, a corrupt government . . . it seems likely we will see a continuation of the process which lost the mainland."[54]

Acheson feared that if the JCS recommendations were adopted, the United States would again jeopardize its prestige with failure. Worse still, the JCS-proposed action probably would unite the xenophobic Chinese in hatred for America. Besides, the Soviets might bring the issue of American interference in Chinese politics to the UN Security Council; before all Asians, the United States and the discredited Nationalist government would be lumped together and roundly denounced. The island's loss, summarized the secretary, could not constitute a breach in America's defense, whereas further association with Taiwan carried a dear diplomatic price.

The day after Acheson's meeting at the Pentagon, the NSC, with Truman's approval, adopted measures and principles in which the State Department's political priorities superseded military ones. Henceforth, American attempts aimed at denying Taiwan to the communists would remain confined to limited diplomatic and economic means. The island's continued independence was charged not to the United States but to "a prompt initiation and faithful implementation of essential measures of self-help by the non-communist administration of the island." Only America's defense perimeter—the Ryukyus, Japan, and the Philippines—was to be energetically reinforced. The NSC

54. *Ibid.*

also reaffirmed its belief that serious Sino-Soviet problems were impending; at the time, Mao and Stalin were meeting in Moscow and declaring, publicly at least, the unshakability of their friendship. The NSC reiterated that the United States should exploit through all available political, psychological, and economic means any apparent rifts between the CCP and Russia and within the Chinese government itself: "Where appropriate, covert as well as overt means should be utilized to achieve these objectives." The concept of supporting indigenous anticommunist Chinese guerrillas was also retained, but with reservations. International law and the United Nations Charter favored the communists against such American-backed activities. More important, the council agreed that mischievous clandestine policies in China could, through their failure and Peking's knowledge of them, jeopardize U.S. intelligence-gathering and propaganda programs in China. Acheson hoped, however, that Pentagon and civilian officials at odds with the prevailing line would be placated by these desperate actions—helping the guerrillas—on behalf of Chinese armies still resisting the PLA.[55]

Designs to woo China away from the Soviet Union in 1949 were based on a sound understanding of Chinese poverty and on the new regime's need to alleviate chaotic civil war conditions, deter famine, and inspire a program of agricultural and industrial development. The administration also relied on the national vitality of the revolutionaries, anxious to deliver China's independence after more than a century of foreign-imposed humiliation. Acheson and his advisers also correctly understood the need not to deflect from the Soviet Union to the United States the fury and anger of a recently liberated people.

Yet the secretary and Policy Planning Staff, including Kennan, underestimated the depth of Chinese resentment toward the United States, resentment fully exploited by CCP ideologues and Soviet-leaning Maoists. The "Open Door" was not understood by politically literate Chinese as an example of American idealism radically opposed to European and Japanese imperialism. Rather, it was seen as a device to guarantee American business interests—imperial latecomers—an equal opportunity for exploiting Chinese markets. Whereas American statements righteously contrasted Washington's altruistic diplomacy with Russia's historic imperial drive, CCP propaganda did not distinguish between American and European/Japanese imperialism. As the influential theologian Reinhold Niebuhr noted soon afterward, "We expect

55. NSC 48/2, December 30, 1949, NSC File, Modern Military Branch, NA.

Asians to be grateful to us for such assistance as we have given them; and are hurt when we discover that Asians envy, rather than admire, our prosperity and regard us as imperialistic when we are 'by definition' a non-imperialistic nation.''[56]

By failing to recognize new China, the administration may have missed a chance to curry favor with Peking's leaders and probably aggravated nationalist tempers, which would otherwise have been somewhat soothed had China been acknowledged as an equal state among others. Washington dawdled too long.

By the end of 1949, administration attempts to delay China's drift toward Russia seemed ironically to promote Moscow's advantage. The selective embargo of goods to China during a period of disruption could only have been understood in Peking as evidence of American ill will. Vital goods, such as petroleum and kerosene, could be and were procured from fraternal Russia. In early December, a Central Intelligence Agency (CIA) report noted that despite considerable inconvenience to itself the Soviet Union was exporting precious, rare kerosene to China to keep Peking's fragile economy intact. Release of the *White Paper*, containing indisputable proof to the CCP of America's deep hostility, meanwhile enhanced the persuasiveness of pro-Moscow Chinese communists over those less enthusiastic about the USSR. Continued, if limited, American aid to Taiwan also confirmed Peking's fears of Washington's interest in Chiang's welfare and constituted unwarranted meddling in the civil war. Peking, too, implicated the United States (unfairly as it turned out) in the Nationalist port blockade.[57]

To make matters worse, the administration had managed, clumsily, to hobble its own diplomacy. Some high officials, by making excessive public statements about the monolithic nature of communism, had inadvertently cultivated a public opinion unreceptive to the subtleties of Acheson's diplomacy. Although the secretary and Kennan publicly discussed prospects for Chinese Titoism, most administration officials, notably the president, referred to indivisible Sino-Soviet bonds and linked the two countries in conspiracy against the free world. Dominant official opinion was typified by an American embassy officer in Moscow who wired Acheson in April that there should "be public assumption no rift is possible" while "we must explore every way and

56. Reinhold Niebuhr, *The Irony of American History* (New York, 1952), 41–42.

57. The official American attitude toward the blockade held that the matter was strictly a Chinese affair. On those occasions when Republican naval ships interfered with American merchant vessels, the State Department issued immediate, curt protests to Taipei. President Truman, however, did not take any steps to curtail or weaken the naval blockade.

means to break the Moscow hold on China.'' As it was, the president had
been slow to understand Acheson's "wedge policy" and all of its implica-
tions.[58]

Truman, by nature a pugnacious man, had little understanding of the deep
causes behind the Chinese revolution and not much more appreciation of the
national aspirations it embodied. He was also personally revolted by the man-
handling and detention of American diplomats by the CCP. In November,
Truman actually proposed to the State Department a program to make $40
million per month available to anticommunist forces on the mainland and on
Taiwan.[59] Acheson and his horrified consultants talked the president out of
the idea and impressed upon him the resilience of the Chinese communist regime and the necessity of eventually coming to terms with it. The president's
farfetched plan was intended in part to overcome critics who lambasted the
administration's China policy; Truman's political concerns did not necessarily prejudice him against Acheson's policy. As leader of his party, however,
Truman was understandably very sensitive to the domestic consequences of
foreign policy. Hence his appreciation of intracommunist problems and the
possibilities they presented to American diplomacy lagged somewhat behind
his clever secretary's.

58. U.S. Embassy in Moscow to Acheson, April 19, 1949, #893.00/4-1949, RG 59, NA;
Dean Acheson, memorandum, "Conversation with the President," November 17, 1949, Acheson Papers.
59. Blum, *Drawing the Line*, 163.

Chapter III

FORMALIZATION OF THE SINO-SOVIET ALLIANCE AND OUTBREAK OF WAR IN KOREA, 1950

American understanding of the two-month-long Sino-Soviet negotiations was sound, based on what is known about them. Both during and after the meetings, Western observers and American diplomats noted signs of strain between the mainland communist leaders. Although American propaganda was robust in publicizing alleged Sino-Soviet problems, the State Department was ineffective, unable to develop much diplomatic leverage. As the year progressed, mutual Chinese-American misperceptions and Soviet and Nationalist pressures on their respective allies helped thwart improved relations between Peking and Washington.

Mao, accompanied by fourteen CCP dignitaries, arrived at Moscow's Yaroslavl railway station on December 10, 1949. There the leader of the most populous nation in the world, who had led one of the most momentous revolutions in history, delivered a brief, modest address. He made polite references to recent CPSU-CCP cooperation, mentioned the need to improve state relations between Russia and China, and alluded to czarist-imposed unequal treaties. Regarding this last, somewhat delicate point, Mao demurely acknowledged, ''After the October Socialist Revolution the Soviet Government, guided by the Leninist-Stalinist policy, took the initiative in annulling the unequal treaties with China which were in force in the time of Czarist Russia.'' The statement was, if nothing else, an indirect suggestion that the Soviets not renege on past performance and, better yet, leave Manchuria and Sinkiang alone, under Chinese sovereignty. The need for economic relief was probably foremost in his thoughts as he next stressed "the strengthening of good-neighborly relations between the two great states of China and the Soviet Union and the development of friendship."[1] In actual negotiations Mao was presumably less oblique.

The Soviets probably realized that they could not manipulate China in the same effective way they did East European states but expected to retain direction of the communist world by recognizing China as a junior partner under Soviet patronage. Mao, eager to obtain Soviet assistance and territorial concessions, praised Moscow's leadership of the international movement and tried to allay Stalin's fears that Peking would follow Yugoslavia's deviationist example. Once in Russia, Mao decried Acheson's attempts to drive a wedge between Peking and the Kremlin. And just before leaving Moscow, the chairman, who usually avoided even the appearance of servility, exclaimed from the train platform, "Long live the teacher of revolution to the whole world, the best friend of the Chinese people, Comrade Stalin."[2] Unfortunately for the future course of Russian-Chinese friendship, Stalin's suspicions were not relieved. Twelve years later, at the Chinese Communist party's plenum in October, 1962, Mao patiently explained, "Even after the success of the revolution, Stalin feared that China might degenerate into another Yugoslavia and that I might become a second Tito. I . . . went to Moscow and concluded the Sino-Soviet Treaty Alliance. Stalin did not wish to sign the Treaty; he finally signed it after two months of negotiations."[3]

The protracted Sino-Soviet meetings resulted in an agreement whereby the Russians promised to surrender control of Port Arthur and the Manchurian Railroad to the People's Republic by no later than 1952. Darien's status as a Soviet naval base remained unchanged and not until May, 1955, was Port Arthur actually returned to China. Mao's request that Outer Mongolia revert to Chinese sovereignty was denied. Instead, both governments swore to guarantee Mongolian "independence," a euphemism for Soviet control.

Reflecting the Soviets' need to rebuild their own war-devastated economy, the Chinese managed to obtain only $300 million in loans, a tiny sum compared to massive American aid given Europe after the war, and trade agreements that, although not unfavorable, did not contain special privileges ei-

---

1. Ambassador Kirk to State Department, December 21, 1949, #802; 761.93/12-2149, RG 59, NA.
2. Perhaps Mao chose the longer, tedious train ride to and from Moscow as a means of preventing any regrettable "accident." See Adam Ulam, *Expansion and Coexistence* (2d ed., New York, 1974), 493.
3. Simmons, *Strained Alliance*, 59.

ther. The niggardly assistance hardly compensated for the $2 billion worth of industrial plant and equipment looted by the Russian army in Manchuria. In addition, Khrushchev suggests in his memoirs that Stalin was especially shameless in his dealings with Mao. Lavrenti Beria, a fellow Georgian and confidant of Stalin's, allegedly provoked his chief's interest in Chinese gold and diamonds and claimed "that there were enormous riches in China, that Mao Tse-tung was hiding them from us, and that if we gave Mao a credit loan he would have to give us something in return." Obviously, the joint Sino-Soviet companies established on Chinese territory for exploitation of mineral resources (oil and mining of nonferrous rare metals) and for air transport were, as Khrushchev admitted, odious to the Chinese. Nonetheless, the limited Soviet loans and trade agreements did help China further its technological development in the 1950s. Also signed at the conference was the Treaty of Friendship, Alliance and Mutual Assistance, providing for defense measures ostensibly aimed against Japan. The underlying concern, however, was with "any other state which should unite in any form with Japan in acts of aggression." Directed against the United States, the treaty's terms were strained in the ensuing Korean War.[4]

According to the American embassy in Moscow, Mao, unlike East European sycophants, did not indulge his hosts with copious homage: "While paying tribute to the leadership of Stalin in world communism, Mao avoids obsequiousness," Ambassador Kirk wrote. Furthermore, most Western observers continued to agree that he did not expect, and would not allow, his country to be relegated to mere satellite status. Yet Mao's position was decidedly difficult. Consul General Clubb wired from China, "Mao stands in danger returning from Russia despoiled of certain sovereign rights and at same time disappointed regarding desire Soviet [to] aid China's hungry masses and shattered economy." The State Department also had evidence that Mao's Moscow visit was pressed upon him by jittery Kremlin leaders fearful that unless they acted swiftly, China would begin an irresistible Westward drift. As it was, Liu Shao-chi and Kao Kang preceded Mao to Moscow. The consul general in Shanghai, Walter McConaughy, guessed that their early arrival indicated Stalin's preference for them.[5]

The precise amount and type of assistance requested by Mao in Moscow

4. Nikita Khrushchev, *Khrushchev Remembers* (Boston, 1970), 463; J.A.S. Grenville, *The Major International Treaties, 1914–1973* (London, 1974), 370.
5. Kirk to State Department, December 21, 1949; *FRUS, 1950*, VI, 288; *FRUS, 1949*, VIII, 639–40.

are still unknown. That he was disappointed is abundantly clear. It has been estimated that the $300 million loan at 1 percent interest granted to China was one-tenth of the total requested; by contrast, Poland successfully negotiated a $450 million interest-free loan from Russia shortly before the Sino-Soviet economic agreements were reached. At the time, some analysts actually wondered if Mao was detained until he accepted Soviet conditions in which commitments compromising Chinese sovereignty and resources were prerequisite to Russian economic aid. Chou Ming-hsun, an agent of communist General Chen Yi and in direct touch during January and February with embassy officials in China, claimed Mao hoped to obtain $5 billion worth of financial help. Extensive capital equipment was needed for the upcoming campaigns in agricultural and industrial production. And apparently military supplies (mostly planes) were required for the planned invasion of Taiwan. Soviet aid, of course, was meager, and by Chou's account it came at a steep political price. As he told Consul General McConaughy, the Soviets wanted in exchange control of Port Arthur, Tsingtao, Che-foo, and Haichow. Chinese "concessions" were also granted to minority groups in Tibet, Sinkiang, Inner Mongolia, and Manchuria. Such concessions, McConaughy adduced, were designed solely to enhance Soviet domination of peripheral China.[6]

From the CIA, the administration received corroborating reports; in January its director, Admiral Bourke Hillenkoetter, wrote a memorandum detailing strong evidence that Peking's leaders had been forced to agree to severe conditions. These included, most conspicuously, China's unconditional lease of Port Darien to Russia. Soviet troops were to be permanently stationed in Sinkiang and the northeastern provinces. In event of Soviet-American war, the Russians were to be allowed use of all Chinese airfields. And in return for Soviet technical personnel and machinery, China agreed to supply Russia with uranium, tungsten, tin, oil, and whatever other products the Kremlin desired.[7] The admiral believed that such provisions, if true, amounted to a Soviet dictate.

In addition to listing Soviet imperial desiderata, a postnegotiations appraisal of the Sino-Soviet treaty prepared for President Truman predicted that China's economic prospects were bleak. The $300 million loan was dismissed as hopelessly inadequate when measured against a background of famine, war desolation, disrupted agriculture, a deteriorating industrial econ-

6. *FRUS, 1950*, VI, 291.
7. Admiral Hillenkoetter, memorandum, January 4, 1950, *Declassified Documents Quarterly*, III (October–December, 1977), 261.

omy, lack of foreign exchange, and a state of semi-isolation. In addition, John Paton Davies advised that "Soviet imperialism will probably become more onerous in its expectations on Communist China [and it] will feel with increasing severity [the] present food shortage and general economic difficulties. The pressure of these events will inspire nationalistically inclined leaders in the CCP to break with those elements in the leadership who have sold themselves out completely to the Kremlin." American propaganda programs consequently took up themes that emphasized Peking's resistance to Soviet demands and Russian stinginess despite projected catastrophic Chinese famine and claimed that Moscow exploited Chinese laborers in Siberia.[8]

Neither official Soviet nor Chinese sources reveal anything about rival groups within the CCP that may have come near to clashing during the Mao-Stalin meetings.[9] But from American documents a tantalizing, if incomplete, impression of Chinese party disquiet emerges. Evidently, Chen Yi, designated commander of the Taiwan liberation campaign, and Liu Po-cheng, commander of the Second PLA Group, were likely military members of an embryonic anti-Soviet coalition of Chinese communist leaders. To Davies, Kennan, and other State Department officials, it therefore seemed sensible to cultivate and judiciously support such nationalistic communists.

In January, Chou Ming-hsun, still on behalf of Chen, was secretly in contact with American officials in Shanghai. He inquired about the possibilities of U.S. aid should an intra-CCP military conflict ignite; the projected struggle would probably feature General Lin Piao against Chen and Liu. It is possible, of course, that Chou's real mission was the opposite of what it appeared and that he sought to spread disinformation and probe American intentions. (Chou was a shadowy figure, about whom little is known.) Such a hypothesis, however, cannot now be proved or disproved. And even if true, there is not a shred

---

8. Policy Information Committee Weekly Review, "Far East: Appraisal of Sino-Soviet Treaty," February 21, 1950, George Elsey Papers; *FRUS, 1950*, VI, 305.

9. Recently there has been a trend among Soviet historians to argue that Chinese communist leaders sought to collaborate with American imperialism in 1949. See, for example, Andrei Ledovsky's article, "Maoist Clandestine Contacts with American Diplomacy in 1949," *Voprosy Istorii*, No. 10 (1980). Relying exclusively on American documents from the *Foreign Relations of the United States* series, the author tries to show that Mao and Chou En-lai were pleased to surrender communist pretensions and policies in exchange for American economic aid to China: "Mao and his closest associates were prepared to go to all lengths to seize political power in the country and strike a bargain with American imperialism for the sake of attaining their selfish aims. This conspiracy was thwarted by the victorious development of the people's revolution which enjoyed broad international support from the forces of democracy and socialism and which relied on the Soviet Union's internationalist assistance." This article, or any others that I know of, does not explicitly mention the 1950 Sino-Soviet negotiations.

of evidence to suggest that the Americans suspected such an ulterior motive. In any case, notwithstanding the dubious "gifts" acquired by Mao in bargaining with Moscow, internecine Chinese party fighting did not erupt in 1950. Except for Kao Kang, who was purged in 1953, "pro-Soviet" Chinese leaders were not dispatched wholesale until the Cultural Revolution. Frustrated American policy makers in late February believed that advocates in China of cordial relations with the United States were in ragged shape: "Any public rumblings of disappointment over the insufficiency of the loan or any demonstrations of resentment against the USSR, the Treaty or the agreements will be quelled forcibly by the Stalinist faction within the Chinese Communist Party, whose position has been greatly strengthened by their conclusion."[10]

More than just the conclusion of Sino-Soviet negotiations hampered administration plans to weaken the communist alliance. The Chinese communist regime in revolutionary impatience sought to reclaim Taiwan as soon as possible; but the administration, though anxious to be rid of the island, was unable to disentangle itself because the Nationalists and their supporters in Congress prevented American withdrawal. In January the administration attempted to drive an important Korean aid bill through Congress. It was almost immediately opposed by a group led by Vorys of the China bloc, southern Democrats, and fiscal conservatives. Not until the administration agreed to extend the China Aid Act ($105 million were unexpended) from February to June, 1950, did the China bloc relent and permit passage of the Korean legislation. Soon thereafter, for similar reasons, the administration yielded again to pro-Taiwan congressional sentiments and advanced the act's expiration date to June, 1951.

These setbacks to the administration's diplomacy are partially understandable when viewed against the increasingly unwholesome domestic political climate of early 1950. From January to March Acheson explained for the edification of American audiences that the Soviets were hell-bent on detaching northern parts of China and were exhausting valuable natural resources in Sinkiang. In this he was assisted by newsmen such as Ernest Lindley, who wrote, "Wrong as it may have been in the past, the State Department is now advocating the only feasible China policy for the future, which is to play for a schism between China and Russia."[11] And through Cyrus Sulzberger of the New York *Times*, the State Department circulated rumors of Soviet attempts

---

10. *FRUS, 1950*, VI, 291; Policy Information Committee Weekly Review, "Far East."
11. *American Opinion on International Affairs*, "January, 1950," Office of Public Affairs, Department of State, RG 59, NA.

to bribe Mao. Still, public attention was focused largely elsewhere. During this period, a Senate subcommittee headed by Millard Tydings was investigating alleged State Department disloyalty cases. Senator McCarthy's shocking charges of communist conspiracy and traitors in the Foreign Service were eventually judged unwarranted by Tydings and his colleagues. Yet the premises underlying McCarthy's allegations (that international monolithic communism threatened the United States and that something wrong was deeply embedded in the foreign policy establishment) were not wholly discredited. Instead, they continued to compete with Acheson's less forcefully expressed views that setbacks abroad were not the result of treachery at home and that differences underlay presumed communist solidarity. In regard to the latter, Acheson often tailored his public comments to disgruntled Chinese predisposed against both their own government and the Soviet Union. The secretary, however, did not reassure the administration's critics and succeeded only in further arousing communist suspicions. Nothing better illustrated Acheson's dilemma than his famous National Press Club address, delivered on January 12, 1950. It drew apprehension and ridicule at home and in Peking.

Acheson justified limiting future aid to Taiwan on grounds that the Nationalist regime had recently received "vast quantities of supplies" and "resources in plenty to buy whatever they might need." The secretary also explained that if and when it became necessary, American aid and military support of Taiwan would be forthcoming. Despite his assurances, many critics later chastised the secretary for not providing sufficient guarantees to Nationalist security. Comments such as "The U.S. has no desire to obtain special privilege or to establish military bases on Formosa at this time" were thought singularly irresponsible. Indeed, one can fairly argue from the tenor of Acheson's speech that Taipei's security was not his first concern. Probably he hoped to signal Peking that America was completely out of the civil war and that Taiwan's final disposition was exclusively a Chinese matter. The island was, if nothing else, beyond the U.S. defense perimeter.

In addition, the secretary worked one of his favorite themes: "The Soviet Union is detaching the northern provinces of China from China and is attaching them to the Soviet Union." This process, he explained, was complete in Outer Mongolia, nearly so in Manchuria, and making rapid progress in Sinkiang and Inner Mongolia. The Soviet annexation of these provinces was the single most important fact in the relations of any foreign power with Asia, especially the United States. He reiterated, "The consequences of this Russian attitude and this Russian action are enormous. They are saddling all those in China who are proclaiming their loyalty to Moscow, and who are allowing themselves to be used as puppets of Moscow, with the most awful responsibility which they must pay for."[12]

Acheson thus continued to play on alleged Chinese fears of Soviet imperialism; but to Peking's communist leaders it seemed that he had made an open-ended commitment to the Taiwan enemy. After all, Washington's aid continued unabated in one form or another, and the secretary retained considerable diplomatic-military flexibility. If and when the United States chose to do so, it could establish a military base on Taiwan. Therefore, whereas Acheson meant to remind Peking of Moscow's inimical intentions and to express the administration's desire to distance itself from Nationalist remnants, his careful words—aimed partly at deflecting domestic criticism—troubled China's leaders. Pen Wen-ying, a communist sympathizer favoring ties to the United States, warned, "If America keeps Taiwan from new regime, it will lose all China itself in terms of goodwill of Chinese people."[13]

Meanwhile, the department received dispatches from its offices in Shanghai, Peking, and elsewhere emphasizing the theme that aid to Chiang was contrary to the critical objective of luring Mao from Russia. McConaughy, for example, cabled from Shanghai that it was incredible that Taiwan's dubious strategic value outweighed the long-term benefits to be derived from exploiting rising anti-Soviet sentiment in China and basic popular goodwill toward America. He insisted in the most urgent manner that further aid and consideration to Taiwan were not worth jeopardizing China's conversion to Titoism.[14]

Two days after Acheson's National Press Club address, the communists, keeping a previously announced promise to requisition official American property in Peking, invaded America's consular compound. Upon learning of Chinese intentions, the State Department had hoped to deter the proposed requisition. First, through the consul general in Peking, Edmund Clubb, the department tried to convince the CCP that such action was illegitimate; Clubb was directed to explain that the compound premises had been granted to the American government under a 1901 protocol and reaffirmed in 1943. Even

12. Thomas Paterson (ed.), *Major Problems in American Foreign Policy* (Lexington, Mass., 1978), II, 323–27.
13. *FRUS, 1950,* VI, 265.
14. *Ibid.*

so, the department was prepared to return glacis property west of the consulate and enter into negotiations for indemnification of the building.

Failing Chinese adherence to the treaty, the administration warned that all official American establishments in China would be shut. James Webb, Acheson's lieutenant, expressed the fears of many officials when he argued, "To capitulate to the demand would invite similar and progressive actions by the Chinese communists against our people and other official property in Peiping and elsewhere in China." Breaking all contact with China, however, was a miserable prospect for "such action on our part might well be playing directly into Russian hands." According to Clubb, the communists did not want to precipitate total American withdrawal. He argued that the new regime hoped to "speed up recognition by such actions . . . taking such profit as possible in process"; but he also worried that party militants were anxious to see America humbled and crippled as much as possible, regardless of international considerations. Clubb therefore advised against publicizing the threatened communist action for even an indirect American challenge to Chinese prestige would aggravate the already serious situation.[15] Meanwhile, with Acheson's permission, he tried to arrange a meeting with Chou En-lai to discuss the issue and prevent it from escalating further. For reasons still unclear, the communists did not allow Clubb to see Chou, and they brazenly occupied a portion of the diplomatic mission on January 14.

To Senators Knowland and Bridges the communist action vividly illustrated the total, irredeemable failure of America's China policy. The administration responded by closing all diplomatic offices on the mainland and evacuating their personnel. To a bewildered Acheson, the seizures demonstrated Peking's unconcern about American goodwill and constituted a flagrant violation of Peking's international obligations. The bulk of evidence also indicates that as a result of the diplomatic humiliations, Truman rejected altogether any possibility of recognizing China. By Walter Judd's account, an infuriated "Harry Truman set down his Missouri-mule foot and said 'Nuts' (and a few other words), 'I won't recognize a bunch of bandits.' It was only the Communists' mistake at that point which prevented their being recognized in 1950."[16]

The Chinese seizure of American property has been traditionally accepted by historians as merely another example of the CCP's rashness; if the seizures served any rational purpose at all, they demonstrated China's hostility toward

15. *Ibid.*, 271–75.
16. Walter Judd, Oral History Interview, April 13, 1970, Truman Library.

America and indifference to recognition by Washington. Some recently declassified materials, though again fragmentary, suggest, however, that seizure of the compound was not simply an ideologically inspired, nationalistic rampage. On the contrary, the action may have been designed, as Clubb speculated, to hasten American recognition. Evidence would also support the notion that local Chinese authorities improperly executed orders and caused unintended, regretted consequences. And the documents suggest other explanations—some overlapping—of the CCP's action.

First, by their expropriation, the Chinese may have strengthened their bargaining position in Moscow. Having demonstrated uncompromising hostility toward the capitalist world's leader, Mao's regime must have looked less Tito-like than ever to Stalin. Another hypothesis, the opposite, proposed by Robert Simmons, holds that an anti-Mao faction of the CCP authorized the consulate invasion so as "to eliminate potential American influence by this . . . act. Whatever the cause of the seizure of American property, it does seem likely that it weakened Mao's overall negotiating position in Moscow, because Peking was now further isolated from possible contact with the West."[17]

Perhaps the seizure was an attempt to increase patriotic sentiments at home and thereby help consolidate the regime's popular standing. Finally, the Maoists might have discounted American recognition entirely and were content to humiliate the United States along with other imperial governments.

Mysterious as the motives behind the Chinese action may be, *post-facto* reports indicate something of CCP factionalism and anxiety over the recognition issue. Clubb stated that the Foreign Ministry was at first dumbfounded to learn that the Americans, unlike the French or Dutch who received similar rough treatment, would break all relations because of the requisition. Once convinced of the administration's seriousness, high-ranking Foreign Ministry officials became edgy and voiced discontent and criticisms over the possible consequences of the seizure. More than other government agencies, the ministry undoubtedly appreciated the value of conjuring up before the Russians—during a period of difficult Sino-Soviet negotiations—the specter of regular China-American relations.

Clubb also explained that the local official in charge of requisition was reportedly dismissed by his immediate superiors for giving the Americans more than their allotted time to evacuate the consulate. If these rumors were true, reasoned Clubb, this unnamed official was probably a victim of larger intra-

17. Simmons, *Strained Alliance*, 94–95.

party squabbles at the top between those for and against maintaining links with Washington. In another report, Clubb contrasted the treatment of the British embassy (it was left alone) with that meted to the American; the British recognition policy perhaps allowed the Chinese to signal other governments that recognition by them would spare their embassies future difficulties. He concluded that whatever China's motives, the regime regretted its action or would soon, as China was becoming increasingly isolated and only the parsimonious Russians were available to relieve famine and economic disorder.[18] As the following episode suggests, by January the Soviets may have already begun to fail their Chinese comrades on other fronts, too.

On January 13, Ambassador Jacob Malik, Soviet representative to the United Nations, proposed that the international body admit the Chinese communist government. An American-led drive dashed the move, and in apparent protest the Soviet delegation began its notorious boycott of the UN Security Council. Some scholars have speculated that Malik's boycott was part of a grander Soviet strategy aimed at isolating China from the West. If the Soviets had been more patient and waited a bit longer before walking out, the majority required for seating Peking could have been mustered; realizing this, the Soviets removed themselves and ingeniously declared that they would disregard any Security Council decisions in which Taiwan's representative was included.[19]

Britain's UN Security Council delegate, Sir Alexander Cadogan, suspected that "the Soviet attitude was based on a calculated policy of discouraging rather than encouraging recognition of the new Chinese government by the United States or France. China could thereby be kept more effectively in isolation from the West and under Soviet domination."[20] Of course, Chinese invasions of foreign diplomatic missions had already diminished Peking's chances of UN admission. (Although the American UN representative publicly claimed in March that he would accept a majority decision on China, the State Department took steps privately to prevent any future majority vote in favor of Mao's government.) Nevertheless, although there is no evidence to suggest that the administration suspected the Soviets of freezing the Chinese out of the UN, Soviet actions, deliberate or not, helped thwart direct Washington-Peking contact. Taiwan's policies at the time also served a similar end.

As previously mentioned, the Nationalist blockade of mainland ports had

18. *FRUS, 1950*, VI, 286–89.
19. Simmons, *Strained Alliance*, 82–95; Tsou, *America's Failure*, 523–27.
20. Tsou, *America's Failure*, 524.

provoked China to blast the United States as responsible for Taiwan's mischief. In January and February, 1950, the Nationalists must have been especially gladdened by the work of their air raids against the mainland. In a scathing indictment, Communist China's press blamed the United States for extensive bombings, which caused more than one thousand casualties and destroyed the American-owned Shanghai Power Company. Communist papers claimed that the bombers were flown by Japanese and American pilots and the destruction of an American company proved that the administration authorized the attacks; the KMT would not otherwise have dared strike American property. Truman's and Acheson's disclaimers that the planes and bombs were not of American origin were disparaged by the CCP and said to illustrate Washington's mendacity and depravity.

Acheson, sickened by the Nationalist use of American-marked planes and outraged by the impact of the raids on popular Chinese opinion, sent sharply worded protests in early February to Nationalist political and military leaders. He condemned the bombings for damaging American property and for endangering the lives of Americans still in China. He fumed that the planes had not been transferred to Taiwan's control for use against nonmilitary institutions and densely populated civilian centers. He also wired the American embassy staff in Taipei that the Nationalist action was ineffective from a military point of view and irrelevant to Taiwan's security. The raids could "only result in inflaming populace against Chinese Government and against U.S. through use of American equipment for such purposes."[21]

Robert Strong, chargé at Taipei, doubted the effectiveness of Washington's protests. Rather, he was convinced that the Chinese Republican navy and air force "both have the idea U.S. will not retaliate in any serious way almost regardless of what they do."[22] He was not far wrong. Despite Acheson's searing disapproval, the raids continued and caused further heavy casualties among Chinese civilians. Possibly this was Taipei's way of demonstrating that, despite Mao's negotiations with the Soviets, Peking still could not ensure external security. In any event, the apparent American connection with the raids seemed a terrible vindication of communist bias against Washington.

The director of the State Department's Chinese Affairs Office, Philip Sprouse, complained bitterly that the United States was arraigned before the bar of Chinese opinion in stronger terms than the Nationalists themselves. He

21. *FRUS, 1950,* VI, 307.
22. *Ibid.*

worried that the chaos caused by the bombings might result in total anarchy and mob acts against Americans on the mainland. Although such unpleasant actions probably would be instigated by local communists, he feared ''the Chinese people as a whole will look upon them as a result of our association with a discredited government, which is indulging in an operation which cannot basically affect the outcome of the struggle'' against the CCP. He could hardly believe that the United States still permitted the Nationalists to damage America's already precarious position in China. He recommended, therefore, that the administration make clear to Chiang that all American aid, military and otherwise, to Taiwan would be stopped if the bombing attacks did not cease. Acheson became so incensed by Taiwan's disregard of American demands to desist and by a note ''telling us to go to hell with our protest on the Shanghai bombings'' that he ordered Assistant Secretary Livingston Merchant to investigate thoroughly the possibilities for breaking with the Nationalists on the basis of their misconduct and arrogance.[23]

Disengagement from Chiang's government (he was formally reinstated on March 1) was politically unfeasible. On February 9, Senator Joseph McCarthy had sparked renewed China bloc impetus by declaring that several score communists worked in the State Department. Among the conspirators was John Service, ''who had previously urged that Communism was the best hope of China.'' A symbiotic relationship quickly developed between the Wisconsin senator and the China bloc's pillars, Senators Taft and Knowland. They offered McCarthy respectability, and he provided dynamism for their seemingly moribund cause. Whereas the bloc previously complained of appeasement and leftist sympathizers in the White House, McCarthy alleged conspiracy and betrayal in explaining the ''loss of China.'' Domestic reaction and the defeated Chiang were neatly knit together when McCarthy charged on March 30, ''It was not Chinese democracy under Mao that conquered China, as Acheson, Lattimore, Jessup and Hanson contend. Soviet Russia conquered China, and an important ally of the conquerors was this small leftwing element in our State Department.''[24] Abiding popular interest in the Tydings subcommittee investigation of State Department disloyalty meanwhile diminished Acheson's hopes of breaking with Taipei. And that March, Chiang's congressional friends managed to extend an unexpended $50 million from the China Aid Act to Taiwan.

Despite varied policy problems, the administration still trusted that de-

23. *Ibid.*, 312–13.
24. Tsou, *America's Failure*, 544.

plorable economic conditions and rising popular frustrations in China would work to America's benefit over the long run. State Department officers also hoped that the Chinese government, pressed by Soviet demands and domestic hardship, might prove amenable to immediate direct talks. After previous thwarted attempts, Clubb met on April 10 with a Chinese Foreign Office official, Lin, to arrange talks with Mao or Chou, but to his chagrin, Clubb's assignment was again frustrated. Lin first excitedly denied that detention of American diplomats Smith Bender and Angus Ward reflected China's contempt of international obligations. Instead, Lin sermonized that the United States's refusal to recognize China demonstrated its disdain for Chinese sovereignty. Finally and most important, he warned Clubb that as long as the United States supported Chiang, an improvement in Sino-American relations was impossible.[25] As for Mao and Chou, Lin explained that they were too busy to meet with any American officials.

The administration still persisted, vainly, in trying to woo Peking. To the utter annoyance of the Defense Department, limited amounts of U.S. oil and West German steel rail were exported to China. And in late April, Truman approved State Department plans to develop a famine relief program for China.[26] The administration was also careful to avoid involvement with Peking's Tibetan adversaries: their requests for military aid were emphatically refused, technically on the grounds that, as in the past, Great Britain and India bore primary responsibility for Tibet's security. Nationalist requests for additional aid, which were supported by American military attachés on Taiwan, were also rejected in April.

By the end of the month CIA estimates that Taiwan would fall to the communists before December seemed nearly confirmed. On April 27, Kuomintang forces were easily dispersed at Hainan Island. Some of the island's defenders defected; a "fifth column" was especially effective. Simultaneously, on Taiwan, the loss of the Chusans was widely anticipated, and those in Taipei who could began hastily to arrange their departures. A few weeks later, before a threatened communist invasion was launched, the Nationalists unexpectedly abandoned the entire Chusan archipelago. America's chargé in Taipei noted that as a result of the Nationalist withdrawal, all PLA resources and attention were concentrated against Taiwan. He estimated that the invasion

25. *FRUS, 1950*, VI, 329.
26. *Ibid.*, 625; Meeting with the president, "Famine Relief for China," April 27, 1950, Box 128, Acheson Papers.

would occur sometime between mid-June and late July.[27] Accordingly, the State Department prepared to evacuate its employees and all American civilians from Taiwan. Plans were also developed for transferring Chiang and his entourage to the Philippines.

In retrospect, it is unlikely that Communist China could have easily launched a successful amphibious invasion of Taiwan at any time in 1950. The Chinese navy was an antiquated little force that was useful for coastal patrol and assault against thinly defended islands but was little match for any larger assignment. As for the PLA, it was well disciplined, endowed with high morale, and staffed by tough, experienced veterans; but it had never invaded large island strongholds, and Nationalist fortifications at Quemoy and Matsu, only a short distance from the mainland, had held earlier in 1950 against communist attacks. There was nothing, then, to inspire confidence that the Chinese communist army and navy could combine successfully to overwhelm a more distant and stronger Taiwan. The exaggerated fears in Washington and in Taiwan itself reflected the degree to which the Nationalists had become demoralized and the despair, felt by Foreign Service officers and State Department officials alike, for Chiang and his cause. The quantity and type of military force the communists could have directed against Taiwan are certainly open to question. Less debatable, though, is that Taiwan in mid-1950 showed many symptoms of defeat and that the administration was anxious to cut its losses, to free itself of the diplomatic and military liability of carrying Taipei. The Korean War, however, as we shall see shortly, changed the attitude of many ranking American civilians toward the island.

During late spring, some State Department officials (notably, Assistant Secretary Dean Rusk and W. Paul Armstrong) devised a plan that would finally deliver the United States from its Taiwan burden. They hoped the United States could persuade the UN Security Council to designate Taiwan as a UN trusteeship. In keeping with this plan, ships of the U.S. Navy would be ordered to prevent any armed attack against Taiwan as long as the move for trusteeship was pending. Yet despite the plan's merit, Rusk worried that "the Russians may welcome a potential commitment of U.S. forces in the protection of Formosa, which would give them an opportunity for pushing the Chinese communists into a clash with us."[28] The interposition of Seventh Fleet ships between Taiwan and the mainland was thus considered before June 25,

27. *FRUS, 1950,* VI, 340.
28. *Ibid.,* 349.

and the danger that the Soviets might precipitate or at least welcome Sino-American fighting was foreseen well before it occurred in Korea.

During the few weeks immediately preceding the start of Korean hostilities, America's China policy shifted, becoming firmer and less flexible. Essentially, the administration had become pessimistic about any early eruption of Sino-Soviet discord and was resigned to the evidence that Soviet sway in China could not be dislodged, at least not in the near future. Just before his departure from China in April, McConaughy reported that three thousand Russian civilians and soldiers had been cheerfully received in Shanghai. He dismissed entirely the possibility of an impending Sino-Soviet break; for the time being a cooperative spirit prevailed between Soviet advisers and their hosts. He added further that the CCP was unlikely to accept American food relief on terms advantageous to the West.[29]

China policy also reflected the dominant themes in the famous NSC 68, proposed in April. Although it mentioned national differences among communist states, NSC 68 stressed the basic compatibility of Marxist regimes and their common policy purpose. Sino-Soviet cooperation, despite some apparent tensions, was held to be basically sound. Furthermore, NSC 68 presented American-communist rivalry as a total contest in which highly coordinated Soviet-communist policy in China directly threatened American interests in the Far East. Reflecting the ideas of its moving spirit, Paul Nitze, who replaced Kennan as head of the Policy Planning Staff in early 1950, this seminal Cold War document stressed the imminent military threat posed by the Soviet Union and international communism. Kennan, by contrast, was convinced that the Soviet Union, though a formidable adversary, was neither capable nor anxious to wage aggressive war. Yet, through NSC 68, Nitze's views prevailed, and containment came to resemble even less the political and economic strategy preferred by Kennan. Within a year of Truman's acceptance of NSC 68—after the Korean War had started—American military manpower increased by one million men, aircraft production quintupled, and the defense budget for fiscal 1951 skyrocketed to $48.2 billion, nearly $35 billion more than originally planned. Not surprisingly, policy toward China reflected somewhat the evolving Pax Americana.

In early June, the administration took measures to curtail seriously the type and quantity of American exports to China. The same principles that gov-

29. *Ibid.*, 353.

erned the export of materials to the Soviet Union and Eastern Europe were applied to trade with China.[30] All 1-A materials were restricted, and additional limits were imposed on 1-B items. And, alarmed that Western petroleum exports to China might find their way to North Korea, the United States halted the sale of American oil to Peking with the advent of fighting in Korea. The administration also convinced the French, Dutch, and Belgian governments to exercise similar control over their companies. Even the British, though ever alert to Hong Kong's precarious position, allowed only a trickle of oil to reach the mainland and discontinued that by late July.

Kennan wrote in his memoirs, "All through that summer [of 1950] I had the feeling that the situation was slipping away not only from the control but from the influence of people like myself." Insofar as policy toward the Sino-Soviet alliance was concerned, Kennan's sense was accurate. The chances for a successful policy based on diverging Soviet and Chinese interests rapidly eroded between July and November. This is not to say, however, that the understanding embodied by previous NSC recommendations and actions was entirely abandoned or that differences between Soviet and Chinese goals were simply ignored. For example, State Department influence was strong enough to restrain the administration from approving JCS plans to bomb Chinese ammunition depots that supplied North Korean and Taiwan invasion forces. Taiwan's offer to send troops to Korea was also refused, partly because such a move would be interpreted in Peking as evidence of continued collusion between Taipei and Washington. In addition, the United States successfully opposed Nationalist plans to bomb PLA concentrations on the mainland opposite Taiwan and the Pescadores. Also, interestingly, Defense Department officials argued that an eventual united democratic Korea might seduce Manchuria away from China, thereby raising doubts in Peking about the wisdom of alliance with Moscow. And, though it may have seemed to Peking that the intrusion of American warships between China and Taiwan constituted decisive, renewed interference in the civil war on Chiang's behalf, Truman's order was as much aimed at preventing Nationalist raids against China as thwarting Peking's invasion plans; the object was simply to check the civil war's escalation and contain the spread of violence in northeastern Asia. Nor did the administration grant any new favors to Taiwan; Truman declared on June 26 to his closest advisers that he would not provide the Nationalists with

30. *Ibid.*, 638–39.

"another nickel." Besides, he gibed, most Nationalist funds were already invested in American real estate.[31]

Although in June, Truman was not committed to retaining Taiwan for the West, fighting in Korea increased his appreciation of the island almost overnight. The Joint Chiefs of Staff, supported by MacArthur, again asserted Taiwan's strategic importance and strongly recommended measures to strengthen the island against invasion. More significantly, Acheson modified his earlier position and convinced the president that American naval action was now required to guard Taiwan, thereby protecting the "sea and air flank of forces operating in Ryukyus-Japan-Korea area."[32]

According to Kennan, the attack by North Korea stirred official Washington "up like a stone thrown into a beehive. People went buzzing and milling around, each with his own idea of what we were trying to do. Nothing seemed more futile than the attempt to infuse mutual understanding of concept, consistency of concept, and above all sophistication of concept into this turmoil of willful personalities and poorly schooled minds."[33] These harsh words may have been aimed at, among others, Secretary Acheson, whose post-June memorandums and speeches were characterized by a hitherto unfamiliar tone. Acheson had long been careful to distinguish Chinese interests from Soviet, but in July he began to speak seriously with high government officials of a Peking-Moscow conspiracy against free nations, of communist timetables, and so forth. Some of the questionable propositions of NSC 68 were obviously taking grip on Acheson, too. As the following episode illustrates, by early July the administration was less willing to act in accordance with earlier adopted plans devised against Russia and China.

On July 10 the administration learned through Indian representatives that negotiation of a Korean armistice would be welcomed by the People's Republic. Chinese support for beginning the talks was contingent, however, on the granting to Peking of a United Nations seat and on restoration of the Korean *status quo ante* by full Security Council participation—that is, the Soviet Union had to be included in UN efforts to end the fighting. The Soviet Union rejected the second half of the two-part plan. And the administration rejected both points, with Kennan in dissent. Kennan felt the opportunity of

31. Kennan, *Memoirs*, 499; *FRUS, 1950*, VI, 403; John Spanier, *The Truman-MacArthur Controversy and the Korean War* (New York, 1965), 69; John Gaddis, "Defensive Perimeter Concept," in Borg and Heinrichs (eds.) *Uncertain Years*, 111; Dean Acheson, memorandum of conversation, June 26, 1950, Box 157, Acheson Papers.
32. *FRUS, 1950*, VI, 391, 396.
33. Kennan, *Memoirs*, 500.

exploiting a Sino-Soviet disagreement had presented itself; he argued at the time that, given the desirability of a cease-fire (in July, 1950, South Korean chances for survival were rated poor), "any efforts being made anywhere to solve the Korean affair" were worth exploring, especially if "they appeared to reveal possibilities of splitting the Chinese Communists from the Russians on issues of real importance." He wagered that the Soviets would be placed in a most awkward position if the United States should suddenly reverse itself and permit China to enter the United Nations according to an agreement whereby Peking would support a Korean armistice along the lines suggested by India. The Soviets would then have to choose between "returning to the Security Council and disagreeing with the Chinese Communists in the UN about Korea or remaining outside the Security Council while the Chinese Communists were in it." Such a situation, he felt, would be very odd and should cause much general embarrassment to the communists. For Kennan, American acquiescence to China's UN admission was not equivalent to recognizing the communist regime; in fact, these were two distinct issues. He maintained that it made no difference whatsoever if People's China entered the United Nations because the United States would not be obliged automatically to establish regular relations with the communist government. He commented, "I hate to see what seems to me a minor issue, on which we should never have allowed ourselves to get hooked in the first place, become something which the Russians can use to our disadvantage in the Korean affair."[34]

John Foster Dulles, then a special adviser on the Japanese Peace Treaty, had a deeper appreciation than Kennan of the domestic political ramifications of supporting a Chinese UN bid. He cautioned repeatedly and persuasively against moves that appeared to suggest a retreat on the Chinese communist issue. By Kennan's account, Dulles maintained that the government would be viewed as "buying some Russian concessions about Korea and that it would therefore seem to our public as though we had been tricked into giving up something for nothing." An embittered Kennan later recalled that Dulles' argument possessed a raw, indisputable force. Kennan subsequently railed in his diary against "the damage done to the conduct of our foreign policy by the irresponsible and bigoted interference of the China lobby and its friends in Congress." Refusal to allow the Chinese into the United Nations seemed to him unforgivable folly and contrary to any realistic assessment of international politics in Asia. It also seemed to "imply that the basis of our policy

34. *Ibid.*, 491–92.

in the Far East from here on out would be an emotional anti-Communism which would ignore the value to ourselves of a possible balance between the existing forces on the Asiatic continent, would force everyone to declare himself either for us (and incidentally Chiang Kai-shek) or against us."[35]

Although Kennan's portrait of Dulles in this episode is unflattering, it does conform to Dulles' general concern for the effect of foreign policy on the electorate. Given his aspirations, it would be compromising if he were associated in the public mind with an unpopular, conciliatory policy toward China.

By the end of August, his policy-making influence chipped away, a sore, deflated Kennan left the administration and ensconced himself at the Institute for Advanced Study in Princeton. This difficult, impatient man, brilliant but not always persuasive, had been unusually perceptive about the true nature of the Sino-Soviet relationship. His absence from the highest counsels of government would be keenly felt in the months ahead, as Truman and Acheson led the nation through tortured policies in Asia.

In late July, General MacArthur, arguably the most esteemed American soldier of World War II, visited Chiang Kai-shek, ostensibly to discuss Far Eastern affairs. An unforeseen consequence of MacArthur's trip was that it initiated his estrangement from the administration, which culminated nine months later in his dismissal.

Administration officials feared that the Chiang-MacArthur consultations created an impression of total American commitment to Taiwan. Indeed, both men made strenuous efforts to project an image of close American-Taiwanese partnership. MacArthur publicly praised the generalissimo's "indomitable determination to resist Communist domination" and added that "his determination parallels the common interests and purpose of Americans, that all people in the Pacific should be free—not slaves." Chiang was no less enthusiastic in paying respects and frankly proclaimed that the two leaders had established a firm foundation for Nationalist-American cooperation. Upon his return to Tokyo, MacArthur arranged for three squadrons of U.S. Air Force jet fighters to be transferred to Taiwan without the approval of Truman or anyone in the Defense Department.[36]

At Truman's behest, Averell Harriman, special assistant to the president, visited MacArthur in Tokyo. There the respected diplomat carefully in-

35. *Ibid.*, 492–95.
36. *FRUS, 1950,* VI, 410.

formed the general of American goals toward China and Taiwan's relation to them. Characteristically imperious, MacArthur in turn eagerly volunteered his own views. He told Harriman that anyone willing to fight communism deserved American support; but as Harriman later reported, MacArthur could not make a convincing case for "why the Generalissimo's fighting would be a contribution towards the effective dealing with the communists in China." Harriman then mentioned the administration's tentative plans for holding UN-sponsored elections on Taiwan to determine its political future. Finally, the president's envoy contrasted administration hopes for a peaceable China-Taiwan resolution with Chiang's desire to use the island as a base from which to launch his invasion of the mainland. MacArthur responded by admitting that without American aid a Nationalist offensive was hopeless and added sarcastically, "It might be a good idea to let [Chiang] land and get rid of him that way."[37]

According to Harriman, MacArthur betrayed a colossal misunderstanding of American aims in East Asia: "He did not seem to consider the liability that our support of Chiang . . . would be to us in the East." In addition, MacArthur objected to administration plans that anticipated eventual recognition of Peking and admission of China into the United Nations after the end of Korean hostilities; he warned that such a misguided course of action would only strengthen Mao's prestige. He recommended that the United States should instead aim at dividing Mao's supporters and encourage internal resistance movements against him. By creating strong dissension and supporting anti-Maoist elements, the United States could still retrieve China from Soviet control. He argued that the United States could have predictable working relations only with a noncommunist China; to think otherwise was the height of naiveté. The general also encouraged Harriman and Truman to threaten Peking if construction of military airfields along the mainland coast continued unabated. As for Taiwan, MacArthur expressed dismay at State Department officials "kicking Chiang around."[38]

After hearing from Harriman of MacArthur's halfhearted support for America's Far Eastern policy, the president directed Secretary of Defense Johnson to reemphasize to MacArthur that his mission was to prevent any Nationalist attacks against the mainland. The general complied with the order but could not resist impudence. He reported to the Pentagon that he understood the decision "to protect the Communist mainland."[39]

37. *Ibid.*, 428.
38. Spanier, *Truman-MacArthur Controversy*, 72.
39. *Ibid.*, 73.

Making matters worse, MacArthur dispatched a message on August 28 to the Veterans of Foreign Wars convention in Chicago (of which numerous copies were sent to newspapers and journals but none to the White House or State and Defense departments) that infuriated the administration. In this report, MacArthur stressed Taiwan's crucial strategic importance to the West and labeled China America's primary enemy in Asia. He also explained, "Nothing could be more fallacious than the threadbare argument by those who advocate appeasement and defeatism in the Pacific that if we defend Formosa we alienate continental Asia." Furthermore, Washington's Pacific allies— Australia, New Zealand, and Japan, as well as Taiwan—needed American protection; alone, they could not successfully oppose "the lustful thrusts of those who stand for slavery as against liberty, for atheism against God." MacArthur concluded his remarks heroically: "The decision of President Truman on June 27 [to intervene in Korea] lighted into flame a lamp of hope throughout Asia that was burning dimly toward extinction." It marked the turning point in the Far East's struggle for freedom and "swept aside in one great monumental stroke all of the hypocrisy and the sophistry which has confused and deluded so many people distant from the actual scene."[40]

The last point was a barely veiled crack against MacArthur's immediate superiors. Truman sensibly reasoned that the message was meant to hinder administration policy by deliberately distorting official judgment on the Far East and committing America to positions unsought by the president. Truman therefore commanded that the general withdraw his message, and MacArthur promptly did so; but it had already been published throughout the nation.

To soften the domestic and international impact of MacArthur's bombast, State Department spokesmen quickly clarified several points for the world press. First, the president, not MacArthur, was the official spokesman on American foreign policy. Moreover, the United States opposed any Nationalist attacks against the mainland, did not have territorial ambitions in China, and was holding in abeyance its decision on the future political status of Taiwan.[41] Thus the administration again tried to alert China that an American-assisted Nationalist invasion was not intended and that Washington was not irrevocably committed to Taiwan.

John Spanier, a historian of the Korean War, writes that MacArthur's "judgment was both unwelcome and unacceptable to the Administration and its allies, since they believed that Mao's regime was potentially friendly to-

40. *FRUS, 1950,* VI, 453.
41. *Ibid.,* 461

ward the West and hostile toward the Soviet Union; they considered that if MacArthur's advice were followed, it would strengthen Sino-Russian bonds instead of weakening them."[42] Spanier's assessment is, of course, broadly accurate, but it is too unqualified to explain fully the ambiguity that characterized administration thinking during the late summer of 1950.

The administration was concerned lest it appear wholly hostile to Peking, and an effort was made to correct the false impression. And yet American policy toward and understanding of the Sino-Soviet alliance was considerably altered in August from what it had been eight months earlier. By late summer a communist division was not considered imminent. As Charles Bohlen told British and French representatives meeting with him in Paris, in some instances "there might be a conflict of [Chinese] national interests with Soviet interests." But one should not expect much. For the most part, he felt that Communist China followed the Soviet line in all questions of international importance and that the United States could thus not reasonably predicate its policy on the vague expectation of a distant Sino-Soviet rift. Besides, such intracommunist problems were "not likely to be brought about by Western attempts to wean Communist China from Kremlin control." In other words, a generous, forthcoming policy would not tempt China to break from the Soviet Union. "If a break should come," he stated adamantly, "it may be expected to come from within," but the West could not hasten the process.[43]

The British representative, Sir Maberly Dening, disagreed and stated that he did not expect China always to play "for the 'beaux yeux' of Russia" when its national interests were involved. He added that Soviet Ambassador Malik's absence from the United Nations was only delaying China's bid for admission by effectively removing the question from the agenda. Dening warned Bohlen that unless Mao was assured of some possibility for constructive relations with the West, he might reach the conclusion that there was no other course than to turn exclusively to the Soviet Union.[44]

The administration, meanwhile, took unfriendly measures against Peking and became more deeply involved in the Chinese civil war. In August, for the first time, financial aid was provided to Tibetan resistance fighters for procurement of weapons; additional economic and military assistance valued at nearly $10 million was also delivered to Taiwan. Understandably, then, nei-

42. Spanier, *Truman-MacArthur Controversy*, 76.
43. *FRUS, 1950*, VI, 420.
44. *Ibid.*

ther China nor Britain had much faith in Washington's concurrent protests that the Taiwan issue should be settled after a Korean armistice. The British did, however, hope that following the November elections Truman would reconsider normalizing relations with Peking. Only Chiang's government paid serious attention to American insistence that Taiwan's ultimate fate was open to future negotiation. Indeed, Taipei officials lived in trepidation that the United States would cut Taiwan off at the earliest convenient time.[45]

India's ambassador to Peking, K. M. Panikkar, reported in late August that the People's Government was convinced that America's ultimate aim was to destroy the new regime. A number of American moves—conclusion of an alliance with Thailand, intervention in Indochina, MacArthur's Taiwan visit, and continued U.S. hostility to Peking's admission to the United Nations—constituted compelling evidence of Washington's cruel intent.[46] Peking also alleged in late August that American bombers had struck three cities (Lin Kiang, Chi, and Talitzu) along the Yalu River. After repeated denials, America's UN representative, Warren Austin, confessed that one plane might have accidentally strafed a Chinese airstrip; subsequent American investigations revealed that a few air raids had been mistakenly conducted north of the Yalu. But despite Washington's proper public apologies and promises of compensation, the Chinese were not placated. Chou En-lai was particularly disappointed that the United States prevented Peking's representatives from attending Security Council sessions that dealt with the bombing complaint. Peking responded by intensifying its anti-U.S. propaganda, and Sino-American relations fell to a new nadir.

Panikkar insisted in early September that China not only desired to avoid fighting in Korea but was also resisting Soviet pressures to attack Taiwan. The Indian ambassador believed that calculated Kremlin-inspired action would push Peking into hostilities against the United States for Soviet ends.[47] In response, Acheson, through the American embassy in India, and Truman, in television and press reports, affirmed anew that the United States was not about to sponsor a Nationalist invasion of the mainland and expressed hope that the United Nations might yet settle the issue of Taiwan's status. American assurances, though, were no more convincing than before, perhaps even less so. After victory at Inchon, American-led UN forces were threatening conquest beyond the Thirty-eighth Parallel, toward China.

45. *Ibid.*, 444.
46. *Ibid.*, 477.
47. *Ibid.*, 480.

Peking's unease was especially evident after Seoul's recapture, which triggered China's release of battle-trained Koreans from Manchuria. Chinese officials also attempted to contact newly appointed Defense Secretary George Marshall, through whom they probably hoped to negotiate withdrawal of the Seventh Fleet and to coax Washington into abandoning Taiwan.[48] Peking also declared for the first time to Panikkar that China could not permit American forces to reach the Yalu River; soon thereafter, Peking publicly broadcast its warning.

Truman and Acheson believed that American victory in Korea and its reunification under UN auspices would demonstrate to Moscow the West's ability and will to resist Soviet proxy aggression. Domestic critics would also be quieted by successful action north of the parallel as proof of the administration's determination against communism. MacArthur, however, stated ambiguously that though he was confident that neither the Soviets nor the Chinese would interfere in the event of American action in the north, he was equally certain that the communists would easily be repulsed by UN firepower if they did dare to intervene. This assessment was hardly reassuring to Truman; despite his desire for military success, he did not want to risk limited engagement with either Soviet or Chinese forces, no matter how few or badly equipped they were. Moreover, the NSC was concerned that the Soviet Union might persuade Peking to enter the war for the purpose of saving P'yŏngyang and "of fomenting war between the U.S. and the Chinese Communists should we react strongly."[49] Consequently, precautions were incorporated into MacArthur's orders on September 2 directing him to invade North Korea.

MacArthur was told that only South Korean troops should conduct operations in the northeastern province contiguous to the Soviet and Manchurian borders. In the event of prior Soviet or Chinese occupation of North Korea, the UN forces should stop at the Thirty-eighth Parallel and continue only "necessary" bombing operations north of that latitude. At this time, the State Department also prepared strategies to seek UN condemnation of Russia, China, or both should they intervene in the fighting.

In mid-October President Truman, distressed by the accidental American strafing of a Soviet air base in the Far East, met with General MacArthur on Wake Island. At the famous conference, Truman sought guarantees that an invasion of North Korea would not precipitate war with Russia or China. The

48. Admiral Hillenkoetter, memorandum for the president, October 5, 1950, *Declassified Documents Quarterly*, III (October–December, 1977), 262.
49. NSC 81, September 11, 1950, NSC File, Modern Military Branch, NA.

overproud general, appearing certain that he understood Oriental psychology and Soviet aims, belittled fears that World War III was in danger of starting. Nonetheless, Truman advised that all due caution be exercised; for MacArthur's benefit he again explained Taiwan's indeterminate status in America's long-range Asian policies and hinted at the desirability of eventually granting a UN seat to Peking. American forces in Korea, meanwhile, continued to roll their enemy north. The communist rout was rapid and, after Inchon, seemingly beyond repair.

Any hopes Peking might have entertained about Soviet intervention were squelched in October in the wake of the UN crossing of the Thirty-eighth Parallel. Virtually all Soviet technicians and advisers fled Korea, with some equipment, to haven in the north near Vladivostok. At the same time, Soviet and North Korean propaganda emphasized that China should act boldly without further delay to restore the integrity of its fraternal, socialist neighbor. By so doing, prated Moscow, Peking would also thwart American attempts to invade China through the Korean peninsula. For its part, P'yŏngyang charged that Japanese soldiers were leading UN forces and, unless stopped, would again perpetrate atrocities against Chinese civilians.

On October 24, the very day MacArthur ordered American troops toward the Yalu, the Chinese People's Volunteers (CPV) were proclaimed and assembled. Volunteers in name only, elements of the Chinese army had already crossed into North Korea at roughly the same time that MacArthur and Truman met at Wake. By conferring the status of "volunteer" on its forces in Korea, the Peking government hoped to avoid legal responsibility for its actions and thereby undermine any legitimacy for American reprisal, military or otherwise, against the mainland. Also on October 24, the PLA advanced into Tibet, probably to secure a perceived weak flank and perhaps to demonstrate for the world China's preoccupation with domestic problems. In the West, however, the Tibet campaign was generally seen as evidence of Peking's aggressive nature and caused an increase in popular American feeling against admitting China to the United Nations.[50]

Mao's war to preempt the feared invasion of vital Manchuria started in late October, when large CPV contingents engaged forward elements of South Korea's First Division and the U.S. Eighth Army. On October 30, when Chinese prisoners were taken, the UN command confirmed reports of Chinese military intervention. In the week following, so-called Chinese volunteers

50. *American Opinion on International Affairs*, "October, 1950," Office of Public Affairs, Department of State, RG 59, NA.

mauled units from both the South Korean and American armies. Then, on November 7, without warning or explanation, the CPV broke contact with the UN forces and even abandoned the hydroelectric complex at Changjin. Two weeks later, the Chinese unexpectedly released more than a score of prisoners. By this gesture, its limited intervention and quick withdrawal, Peking may have meant to indicate China's readiness for negotiations.

Both American and UN spokesmen responded by issuing statements that the Chinese border was inviolate and the West did not harbor designs on Manchuria. With an eye to Soviet pressures on China, Truman remarked that if America's peaceful intentions were misunderstood by Peking's leaders, "it can only be because they are being deceived by those whose advantage it is to prolong and extend hostilities in the Far East against the interest of all Far Eastern people."[51] Still, to the Chinese, U.S. actions mattered more than grand statements. While Peking's representatives were invited to discuss the Korean issue at the United Nations, MacArthur's forces remained dangerously poised along the Manchurian border. Chinese spokesmen complained about America's aggression in Taiwan and recurring violations of Chinese air space and charged that the United States was preparing to invade Manchuria. The Chinese observed, too, that Senator Knowland had proposed a neutral zone ten miles north of the Yalu.

From its standpoint, undoubtedly Peking had sound reasons to fear that the Americans were not bound by their words. UN leaders had originally claimed that their armies would not cross the Thirty-eighth Parallel. Later, they were supposed to stop 150 miles north of it. Later still, only South Korean troops were to continue beyond the waist and were in any event to stop below the Yalu area. Then, on November 24, Peking's worst fears materialized: MacArthur launched his campaign to "bring the boys home by Christmas" and end the war.

Truman probably felt at this point that he had little choice but to accept MacArthur's promises to end the war swiftly, without drawing China into it. The president was keenly pressed for military victory by Taft, whose party had dealt the Democrats heavy losses at the November polls. Both the State Department and Acheson were also under intense fire from critics to demonstrate their resoluteness against Russian imperialism.

Through November 26, MacArthur's confidence seemed justified, as UN forces speedily approached the Yalu and encountered only mild resistance.

51. Spanier, *Truman-MacArthur Controversy*, 120.

On the twenty-seventh, however, the CPV counterattacked, divided Mac-
Arthur's overextended forces, and precipitated the greatest American military retreat in history. A new war had tragically begun. By the first week in
December, MacArthur reported that most of his American troops were
"mentally fatigued and physically battered." The effectiveness of Korean
soldiers was all but dissipated. Amid press dispatches exonerating his own
action and calling for a blockade and bombing of the mainland, MacArthur—
and the JCS—considered evacuating all American forces from Korea. And
to the horror of Washington's European allies, Truman, perhaps in sheer des-
peration, mentioned publicly on November 30 that the use of atomic weapons
in Korea was under serious review.

The British considered Washington's flaunting of atomic bombs both pre-
posterous and dangerous. Dreading general war and uncertain of what the
United States might do next, Prime Minister Clement Attlee journeyed to the
United States in early December for consultation with his intemperate
partner.

During the ensuing meetings, both state executives and their advisers exchanged essentially conflicting views on managing the Sino-Soviet alliance.
But Americans and Britons did agree on two points: that war between China
and the United States would help only the Russians and that, given the distinct long-term possibility of general war against Russia, America's military
strength should not be too long engaged in Korea. It was an indecisive theater
in which the Americans could be bottled up, and the attrition rate was bound
to be high.

To Attlee, the really distressing issue was that the Americans lacked elementary understanding of the Chinese viewpoint. In a meeting on December
4, he stressed that Peking's attitude generally included a large element of fear,
"a genuine fear of the U.S. and of the European nations." He also suggested
that as long as the CCP continued to enjoy success in China, Mao and his
colleagues would be relentless in seeking China's admission to the United
Nations: "They want to have the fullest position of any Chinese government
in recent times. They feel strongly about Formosa and less strongly about Korea."[52] As for Sino-Soviet relations, he doubted that the Chinese wanted to
throw themselves wholly into the arms of Russia. Instead, he felt that China
under Mao would seek to build up its own strength and would pursue independent lines in both domestic and foreign politics.

52. State Department, memorandum of conversation, December 4, 1950, *Declassified Documents Quarterly*, I (January–March, 1975), 29.

Acheson answered, in retrospect incorrectly, that the Chinese armies in Korea received substantial Soviet support. And Truman explained that Peking was simply a Russian satellite, not any different from P'yöngyang. The secretary added that if Washington gave in on Taiwan and permitted China to enter the United Nations while its forces were reeling before strikes from the CPV in Korea, American prestige in the Far East would suffer a grievous setback; as a result, Far Eastern states would rapidly come to whatever terms were possible with Moscow and Peking. To avoid such a setback, said Acheson, the West should stand firm in Korea and on Taiwan.

After a long recital of real and potential Sino-Soviet problems, Attlee questioned the next day "if it was wise to follow a policy which without being effective against China leaves her with Russia as her only friend." Acheson replied by praising Attlee's analysis but doubted that effective action logically followed from it. Besides, added Truman, Taiwan "was quite a political issue in the United States since Chiang [had] many converts here." Attlee responded somewhat haughtily that in Great Britain Chiang enjoyed virtually no support on the question of Taiwan or any other issue. More to the point, Acheson argued: "If in taking a chance on the long run future of China [that it break with Russia] we affect the security of the United States at once, this is a bad bargain especially if our security would be affected by the influence of these steps on Japan, the Philippines and other countries."[53] Perhaps fifteen years hence, Peking would be less hostile to the West, but he cautioned that this was a very long-range view and irrelevant to immediate problems. Indeed, interjected General Marshall, Peking might invoke its treaty with Russia against UN armies in Korea. Acheson then estimated that at least ten years were needed before the American people could accept the idea of rapprochement with China; until then, the path would be difficult.

During the Attlee-Truman talks, the NSC considered both imposing a multilateral trade embargo against China and freezing all Chinese financial assets in the United States. Partly out of deference to the British, who remonstrated that such a move would be understood as a step toward general war, the notion was temporarily dropped. The Commerce Department nonetheless enacted measures to assure that goods of strategic value did not reach the mainland; new, stricter licenses were also required of all American firms dealing with China. A short time later, the JCS was appalled to learn that some American goods providing "aid and comfort" were still being exported to "Com-

53. State Department, memorandum of conversation, December 5, 1950, ibid.

munist China, at a time when that nation is militarily attacking U.S. armed forces." Consequently, on December 16, Truman adopted a policy of comprehensive economic sanctions.

Throughout this period, the State Department was still not completely willing to dispense with diplomacy. A spokesman publicly announced on December 16 that regular Sino-American economic relations should be feasible in the future. But as long as Chinese communist leaders subordinated themselves and their country to international communist imperialism and followed an aggressive policy in Korea, the United States had no choice but to take economic measures against the People's Republic: "If the Chinese Communists choose to withdraw their forces of aggression and act in conformity with United Nations principles, this Government will be prepared promptly to consider removing restrictions and restoring normal trade relations."[54] This statement and others like it were meant to encourage Chinese acceptance of a UN-mediated cease-fire to be negotiated at Lake Success.

Peking's leaders unfortunately refused the invitation to discuss either Korea or Far Eastern problems in general. Chou demanded that before negotiations commenced, all foreign troops must be withdrawn from Korea, American ships evacuated from the Taiwan Straits, and China accorded permanent UN representation. Defiant and victorious, Peking believed it had no reason to accept terms short of complete socialist victory in Korea. In view of subsequent events that will be reviewed later, Peking may have lost a great political victory when it later decided to send its forces south of the Thirty-eighth Parallel.

China's Korean intervention was not only the most palpable expression of Peking's distrust and fear of the United States; it also consummated America's failure to draw China away from the Soviet Union. More than twenty years elapsed before the United States again sought accommodation with Peking to balance Soviet political and military influence in the Far East.

During the war's early phase, the administration pressed China hard and was prepared to inflict heavy casualties on CPV forces in Korea, despite qualms about the diplomatic gains that would accrue to the USSR. Detection and support of indigenous anticommunist Chinese guerrillas were also vigorously

54. NSC 92, December 4, 1950, NSC File, Modern Military Branch, NA; *FRUS, 1950*, VI, 680; Department of State Press Release, December 16, 1950, Office of Public Affairs, RG 59, NA.

promoted for the first time. Furthermore, the United States redoubled efforts in January, 1951, to slow Chinese occupation of Tibet; complaints were filed at the United Nations, and direct American aid in the form of weapons shipments for Tibetan resistance was increased.[55]

By the year's end Chiang had become adept at playing MacArthur in Tokyo and Washington as two separate competing entities. By insinuating himself into MacArthur's favor, Chiang involved himself even deeper than before in American politics and with the administration's domestic opponents. Before them the administration was obliged to bend somewhat and reluctantly granted additional aid to Taiwan. Yet State Department attitudes toward Taiwan and the Sino-Soviet alliance generally altered in late 1950, irrespective of pressures to defend Taipei.

A longtime advocate of dividing China from Russia, Walter McConaughy, like Acheson, believed by December that to yield under Chinese pressure and to oblige Peking with an important concession such as Taiwan would confirm the Maoists in the effectiveness of their aggressive policies, increase their contempt for American military power in East Asia, and embolden those people in the CCP who advocated intimate association with Russia. Concessions to China, then, could not help woo it from Russia but would almost certainly strengthen existing bonds between the two communist states. He believed that not until communist victories in Asia were checked was there "any conceivable hope of convincing [the] Chinese Communists [that] it is not to China's advantage to hitch their wagon to the Russian star." He therefore recommended that ample economic, military, and political pressure be brought to bear against China to force either a change in the leadership's personnel or, more realistically, "decisively demonstrate to them that fighting Russia's battles can in the long run only bring disaster to CCP and China."[56]

Both McConaughy's views and Acheson's comments to Attlee illustrate that the Americans had little sense of China's peculiar reasons for crossing the Yalu or her Korean-related difficulties with Russia. Neither Soviet orders nor excessive concern for P'yöngyang were sufficient reasons for the CPV's offensive. More likely, Peking responded to a perceived, direct security threat as American troops approached valuable, vulnerable Manchuria. Nevertheless, McConaughy's and Acheson's remarks are significant beyond what they

55. *FRUS, 1950*, VI, 598–609, 618.
56. *Ibid.*, 605.

reveal about American misperceptions: the essence of Washington's policy developed from the end of 1950 through 1955 was that military and economic pressure against China could hasten the communist alliance's demise or at the very least reduce its vitality.

Chapter IV

WAR AND TRANSITIONS
1951–1953

The history of the Korean War from early 1951 onward is dreary, marked by inconclusive, costly combat and protracted, frustrating armistice negotiations. Not until July, 1953, was the issue more or less resolved and the antebellum status quo restored. That same year, two other important transitions occurred affecting Sino-Soviet-American relations: Stalin died, and in Moscow there ensued a lively struggle for succession. And in Washington, D.C., Eisenhower and Dulles assumed office, thereby ending two decades of rule by the Democratic party.

During this period, 1951–1953, official American understanding of the Sino-Soviet alliance was more sophisticated than is generally recognized. In particular, American judgments were not handicapped by Dulles' allegedly moralistic-legalistic view of global politics. Meanwhile, the United States took an increased interest in communist activities in French Indochina and accepted a greater responsibility for events in that region.

SINO-SOVIET COOPERATION IN KOREA
AND AMERICA'S RESPONSE

A tantalizing hypothesis holds that the North Korean invasion of the South was prematurely and probably accidentally launched by an overanxious Kim Il-sŏng, catching both Moscow and Peking unprepared. True or not, most evidence now available suggests that China's leadership at least was surprised (the proposed invasion of Taiwan, which faced a host of other obstacles anyway, was indefinitely postponed) and throughout the war resented in-adequate Soviet consultation over an issue decided near important Chinese industrial and population centers. Mao also probably had reservations about communist strategy and may have concluded that Soviet wartime leadership was inept.

Although not expressed until the 1960s, Peking's public assessment of the war cited several counts that demonstrated Chinese moral and political su-periority over the USSR. The riskiness of waging conventional war against the stronger, better-endowed West was illustrated by the near fiasco wrought by United Nations forces; but when forced into such combat, China's army proved capable and prevented disaster while the Soviet army stood idle. Even as American-led forces crossed the Thirty-eighth Parallel, headed toward the Soviet and Chinese borders, Moscow assiduously avoided any provocative moves while repeatedly urging Chinese intervention. Only the successful ac-tion of Chinese "volunteers" saved North Korea's regime.

In addition to providing paltry leadership, the Kremlin proved itself to be ungenerous in supplying materiel. Soviet-supplied weaponry was obsolete and little match for American military technology. Even worse, the Soviets un-graciously demanded and received full payment on all equipment "bor-rowed" by the CPV. China, then, sacrificed thousands of lives and much treasure on a war from which the Soviet Union, which was largely respon-sible, was completely spared. After Sino-Soviet disagreements burst in the 1960s, one of the important charges leveled by Peking was against Moscow's miserliness during the war. A May 9, 1964, editorial in *People's Daily* com-plained about Soviet insistence on collecting loans from China, "most of which were used in the war to resist U.S. aggression and aid Korea. Thus, even the war materiel supplied to China in a war to defend Korean socialism has not been given gratis." During the war itself, Chou En-lai publicly expressed less than full satisfaction with Soviet shipments of supplies, military and other-wise.[1]

True to form, Soviet press and radio commentators have, of course, em-phasized the superabundance of Russian aid during the war. Still, no matter how self-serving or imprecise post-1963 Sino-Soviet polemics may be, they do indicate the nature and seriousness of problems traceable to the Korean War. Even in 1951 many American observers predicted that Peking's re-

1. Hawkins to secretary of state, November 28, 1952, #793.11/11-2852, RG 59, NA.

sentment against the Soviets would grow; as Chinese casualties soared, Stalin merely gave cries of encouragement and some guns.[2]

However disappointed China's leaders may have been in the Soviets, the war naturally confirmed their fears of a ferocious, American-led capitalist camp. From Peking's perspective, the change in American policy toward the Chinese civil war from limited involvement to direct interference (the interposition of Seventh Fleet ships between the mainland and Taiwan) and subsequent clashes in Korea strengthened worst fears about Washington's long-range intentions. Increased economic and military aid to Chiang also helped to reduce drastically the possibility of Sino-American rapprochement in the near future.

America's miscalculation in gauging China's profound sense of strategic insecurity by crossing the Thirty-eighth Parallel resulted in actions that further estranged the two states. United Nations estimates of Chinese slain in Korea number near 900,000 men; the United States suffered 142,000 casualties, including 33,600 dead. Furthermore, to Peking, MacArthur's recommendations for extending the war to China's mainland surely were significant, not because they helped lead to his dismissal but because they reflected a powerful current in American opinion that in the future might dictate Washington's behavior. The repatriation-of-prisoners issue—many thousands of released Chinese and North Korean prisoners of war chose to remain in South Korea or settle in Taiwan—was also a stunning propaganda victory for the West and caused deep resentment in Peking. As it was, the propaganda-conscious revolutionaries were angered by the American-initiated UN resolution that labeled China "aggressor." The international disapprobation merely exacerbated China's sense of diplomatic isolation and strengthened the argument of those CCP members who advocated closer ties with the one country capable of deterring full-scale American assault. Truman shared a similar understanding and judged that if MacArthur's plans were realized, Russia would join the battle. Actually, based on what is now known about the state of Sino-Soviet relations during the war, it is doubtful that Moscow would have risked full-scale war on China's behalf. Better than anyone else, Kremlin leaders knew that war against the United States would end in Russia's decimation.

Soviet leaders must have been delighted by the disastrous condition of relations between Peking and Washington. As a result of Sino-American fighting in Korea, the Soviets acquired considerable diplomatic leverage; and Sta-

2. Ambassador Austin, memorandum to Dean Rusk, May 23, 1951, *Declassified Documents Quarterly*, VII (January–March, 1981), 105.

lin's apprehensions that China could seek a Tito-like path through the Cold War were at least temporarily allayed. China was an international pariah, unrecognized by the United States, rebuffed at the United Nations, condemned as aggressor. Its only possible source of desperately needed aid was the Soviet Union. Irrespective of Peking's disappointment about modest Russian assistance during the war, Soviet leaders knew that Mao realized there was no suitable alternative to alliance with Moscow. In the words of a U.S. diplomat in late 1953, "Mao Tse-tung certainly comprehends the importance of Soviet assistance during the present difficult economic period in Communist China."[3] To the detriment of Peking's interests, Soviet spokesmen during the succeeding decade also acted as chief interpreters of Chinese views to both the United States and the United Nations.

The American view of China was undergoing considerable revision. Before the Korean conflict, the administration perceived the Soviet Union as the main menace to Western interests in Asia; containment of Soviet power necessarily included China, a likely agent of Soviet expansion. The Korean War, though, seemed to demonstrate that China itself was an aggressive, hostile state. Harold Macmillan recorded in his diary at the time of Chinese intervention, "I am very skeptical indeed that China can be detached [from the Soviet Union] by kindness."[4] As we have seen, the Briton's assessment was entirely shared by President Truman and Secretary Acheson.

The mistreatment and alleged brainwashing of American prisoners infuriated public opinion in the United States and seemed compelling evidence of communist barbarism. The bitterness felt by many citizens over the abuse of these men supplemented the China lobby's propaganda that depicted in lurid terms the inhumanity of Mao and his colleagues. "Human waves" thrown against American artillery positions were also cited as proof of communist callousness toward life. These charges complemented the conventional Occidental wisdom that life in Asia is cheap. The enormous size of the "waves" also conjured up images of the proverbial yellow peril, now tinted red, that threatened to overwhelm the democratic West. More fuel was thus added to the fires of an emotionally overwrought anti-PRC campaign. At the same time, as more than one U.S. diplomat ruefully acknowledged, China's Korean intervention raised Chinese prestige throughout the developing world and especially in Asia: "The informed Asian, whatever his attitude toward com-

---

3. Consul general in Hong Kong to secretary of state, September 30, 1953, #793.11/9–3053, RG 59, NA.

4. Harold Macmillan, *Tides of Fortune* (London, 1969), 328.

munism, can hardly have overlooked the fact that Chinese armies fought to a standstill the forces of the most powerful nations of the Western world."[5]

In the United States the war accomplished the long-standing goals of the China lobby. Truman froze all Chinese financial assets, established a total embargo of the mainland, and banned all American ships and citizens from the People's Republic. The United States also became the staunchest bulwark against Peking's admission to the United Nations. American policy toward China during and after the Korean War was not, however, dictated solely by public passions. Through Ambassador Kirk in Moscow, the United States discreetly maintained channels of communication with the Chinese communist government.[6] And the administration did not assume a total harmony of Sino-Soviet wartime interests. During the war's early phase, the administration based its policy on assumptions that tensions existed between Moscow and Peking. Acheson declared in early September, 1950, that Chinese intervention would be sheer madness because of the threat of "a great cloud from the north, Russian penetration."[7]

The administration's later surprise and distress at China's attacks in October and November were explained in terms of essential Sino-Soviet incompatibility; Truman claimed that China had been "forced or deceived into serving the ends of Russian colonial policy in Asia." Several months later, America's ambassador to Taiwan, Karl Rankin, was still confident enough to say, "Among those who know and understand China there is a strong belief that the traditional pride and independent spirit of the Chinese people will, in the long run, triumph over every foreign attempt to dominate them," especially the Soviet attempt. Rankin therefore felt that America's mission was to enlighten the Chinese people, through every means possible, about the true nature of Russian intentions. And neither Rankin nor most other American officials were inclined to charge Chinese collaboration with the June attack by North Korea.[8]

In July, 1951, the State Department understood that Moscow and Peking disagreed about the timing and nature of Korean armistice negotiations. At the time, Chinese internal propaganda was emphasizing the need to raise more money to purchase tanks, planes, and munitions. Soviet Ambassador Malik's

5. Consul general in Hong Kong to Secretary of State, September 30, 1953.
6. Ambassador Kirk to secretary of state, June 22, 1951, #611.93/6–2551 59, NA.
7. Morton Kaplan, *The Life and Death of the Cold War* (Chicago, 1976), 188.
8. Karl Lott Rankin, *China Assignment* (Seattle, 1964), 104; Colonel Stanton Babcock, memorandum for Dulles: "Chinese Communist Participation in Military Operations in Korea," undated, Box 47, Dulles Papers.

concurrent armistice proposal in the United Nations was not readily acknowledged or welcomed in Peking. Dean Rusk, assistant secretary for Far Eastern
affairs, told the Senate Foreign Relations Committee that the Chinese press
carried only one brief reference to Malik's proposal, and that a full forty-eight
hours after it had been issued. Rusk explained further that although Peking
publicly supported the Soviet plan, the Chinese press never demonstrated any
enthusiasm for it and claimed that Americans could have had peace "long
ago if they had accepted in their entirety the [earlier] proposals of the Chinese
Communists." He concluded that the Soviets, unlike their partners, were
willing to settle for a negotiations agenda that excluded both the issues of Taiwan and Peking's admission to the United Nations. The administration, of
course, also preferred not to mix such problems with the Korean armistice
discussions.

During the same summer, 1951, General Matthew Ridgway sent his communist counterpart a cleverly worded invitation for peace talks designed at
least in part to exacerbate Chinese-Soviet differences. Rusk reported, "We
decided not to address it either to the Chinese or North Koreans." Although
the Americans knew who commanded the Chinese forces and who commanded the North Korean units, there was some uncertainty about who was
chief and who was deputy of the communist armies. Rusk continued, "We
also weren't sure we would not stir up a bit of a problem between Peiping and
Moscow."[9] (As it turned out, the reply to Ridgway's offer was signed by
General Peng Ten-huai, who led the Chinese "volunteers" in Korea, and
Premier Kim Il-sŏng.)

Not only during the sporadic peace negotiations but throughout the Korean
War, the Truman administration never lost sight of its long-term goal: to spoil,
or at least damage, the Sino-Soviet alliance. Although the People's Republic
was lost to the West, Soviet advantage gained by alliance with China had to
be reduced. In May, 1951, the NSC enunciated several critical objectives of
which the first was to "detach China as an effective ally of the U.S.S.R. and
support the development of an independent China which has renounced
aggression." To this end the government adopted several measures. It sought
to weaken Peking's leadership by inflicting the heaviest losses possible on
Chinese forces in Korea and held the vague hope of eventually installing a
noncommunist leadership. The administration further resolved to continue its
support of opposition groups sympathetic to the West, including indigenous

9. *Executive Sessions of the Senate Foreign Relations Committee*, III, 543–45.

antiregime guerrillas. The NSC also sought to cultivate China's economic isolation by tightening the economic embargo, opposing her entrance into the United Nations, and encouraging UN political and economic sanctions. In the words of Walter McConaughy, then consul general in Hong Kong, "The point has now been reached where additional [Chinese] dependence on the Soviets for economic necessities is more likely to work in our favor than against us by hastening the day when China becomes disillusioned with Russian aid. Only [when] the Chinese become convinced that they have more to gain from rapprochement with the West than from continued dependence on the USSR will they be in a mood to loosen ties with Russia." [10] Hence the need for stern measures by the United States.

American attempts to isolate China were moderately effective, and certainly actions against its army in Korea were bloodily impressive. French intelligence sources in touch with U.S. officials were convinced, moreover, that the war was extremely unpopular in China, that veterans of the Korean fighting were fully weary of it by 1952, and that the burden of war was weighing heavily upon the Chinese communist government. [11] But efforts at displacing Mao's leadership by aiding anticommunist Chinese forces were too haphazard, too insignificant, to influence Peking's domestic politics. A February, 1951, Joint Intelligence Committee report on the activity of anti-CCP guerrillas estimated that between six and seven hundred thousand irregulars were engaged against Peking. About half were loyal to Chiang; the others were merely traditional dissidents: brigands, warlords, scattered ethnic rebels. These armed groups, which were most active in south and central China, did require considerable PLA attention, and periodic uprisings of disgruntled civilians also plagued the regime. But unhappily, the native antiregime forces, for all of their zeal and industry, lacked coordination, discipline, or even unified purpose. Their campaigns fizzled before the Americans could help develop an effective Chinese resistance.

American propaganda, though, was ever lively. Recurring themes in Voice of America (VOA) broadcasts to China included Soviet perfidy, the unequal terms of the February, 1950, treaty, the shame of "Soviet Manchukuo," Peking's abject obedience to Moscow, and China's costly sacrifices in a war fought for selfish Soviet ends. One VOA program obligingly relayed to its listening audience in China remarks made by Rusk in the spring of 1951 in

10. NSC 48/5, May, 1951, NSC File, Modern Military Branch, NA; Walter McConaughy to secretary of state, September 17, 1951, #793.11/9-1751, RG 59, NA.
11. Achilles to secretary of state, August 1, 1952, #793.11/8-152, RG 59, NA.

which he dismissed the territorial integrity of China as an ironic phrase: "The movement of Soviet forces into Sinkiang, the realities of 'joint exploitation' of that great province by Moscow and Peiping, the separation of Inner Mongolia from the body politic of China, and the continued inroads of Soviet power into Manchuria under the cloak of the Korean aggression mean in fact that China is losing its great northern areas to the European empire which has stretched out its greedy hands for them for at least a century." Underequipped and overtaxed, the Chinese forces and people were being cruelly duped by Moscow. Rusk further lamented that "hundreds of thousands of Chinese youth are being sacrificed in a fiery furnace, pitting their waves of human flesh against the fire power of modern weapons—and without heavy equipment, adequate supply or the most elementary medical attention." He finished by charging that aggressive actions abroad were designed to distract the attention and energies of the Chinese people from Soviet imperial encroachments upon China itself.[12]

The actual impact of these efforts to weaken the Sino-Soviet alliance during the Korean fighting is difficult to assess at present. It is clear, however, that the result of China's imposed isolation was, as the Truman administration expected, an increased dependence on Moscow, which supplied its ally in a grudging and minimal fashion; the majority of CPV arms were of an earlier American vintage or else captured with UN soldiers during the fighting. Some foreign observers also noted strains between the Soviets and Chinese. At one point during the war, in 1952, India's Panikkar declared that "Peking is drifting away from Russia." He was not especially liked by U.S. diplomats, however, and they generally viewed his comments with skepticism, even disdain: "It must be kept in mind that Panikkar tends to abound in his own egoism in conversation, which frequently reduces his reliabilty as a reporter."[13] Although most Peking-based European diplomats were also inclined to reject Panikkar's assessment, they generally did agree that a war-inspired resurgence of Chinese nationalism was causing some problems for Russia. In Tientsin, for example, all shop signs in foreign languages, including Russian, were removed. Furthermore, all foreigners, including those with Soviet passports, had to produce Peking-issued identity papers on request from Chinese officials. Numerous Soviet citizens were caught in the bureaucratic snare and duly punished.

12. Dean Rusk, Address to China Institute Dinner, May 17, 1951, Truman Papers.
13. Ambassador Erik Boheman (Sweden) to Dulles, January 25, 1952, Box 52, Dulles Papers; Harrington to secretary of state, July 14, 1952, #793.11/7-1452, RG 59, NA.

Soviet military and civilian advisers stationed in various Chinese cities also often made poor impressions on their hosts. In Shanghai, according to McConaughy, Soviet cadres fell into three categories: "inefficient, arrogant, or too valuable to be spared by the USSR." Apparently the competent stayed in China only a brief time before Moscow decided that their services were required back in Russia. Especially obnoxious Soviet personnel were also withdrawn, "leaving the inefficient groups who usually knew less than the Western-trained Chinese, but who were invariably better paid." [14] McConaughy surmised that resentment against the Russian guests ran high even among CCP members, who felt that the local residents were being improperly used so that the Soviets in China could maintain a lavish standard of living.

In Peking there was also indications of growing anger among university students and younger communists against Soviet technicians and advisers, who displayed "know-it-all attitudes," were often inept at their tasks, and failed to participate fully in the war effort against U.S. imperialism. McConaughy reported that in several instances the Soviets had to have armed protection against the local populace; and whenever a Soviet citizen was implicated in serious crime, such as rape, it excited popular animosity to an alarming degree. [15]

The Chinese, more significantly, did not attempt to conceal their devotion to their own leaders, particularly Mao, and neglected to pay obeisance to "international" Soviet leaders during state-sponsored rallies and parades. During public demonstrations, even Sun Yat-sen's portrait preceded those of such European socialist luminaries as Marx, Lenin, and Stalin. Unbridled expressions of national pride actually prompted the Soviet ambassador in Peking to declare in an unguarded moment that the Chinese rulers were not real communists but "sheer capitalists."

U.S. intelligence reported that China, engaged against the United Nations and dependent on Soviet assistance, was by no means a reliable long-term Moscow subordinate and that the Soviet creation of a buffer zone out of Sinkiang, Outer Mongolia, and northern Manchuria suggested Moscow's distrust of the future direction of Chinese expansion. The American embassy in Paris also informed Washington that some French businessmen who had recently resided in Shanghai were convinced that Mao and Chou En-lai were chafing under the Russian yoke and would emulate Tito's example if condi-

14. McConaughy to secretary of state, January 6, 1951, #793.00/1-651, RG 59, NA.
15. Consul general in Hong Kong to secretary of state, August 26, 1952, #793.11/8-2652, RG 59, NA.

tions permitted. At one point during the war, American sources reported the rumor that Mao, recuperating from an illness in the Western Hills near Peking, was actually being held captive by his accompanying Soviet adviser, who alone controlled a vast network of communications in China.[16]

From Peking's perspective, probably the only instance of truly vile Soviet misbehavior occurred in 1953, after Eisenhower implied that he would use atomic weapons against China if a Korean truce was not signed. Russia's leaders did not hurry to champion their ally's cause. Indeed, the contrary seems true. The post-Stalinist leadership pressed Peking to end the war quickly and sign an armistice.

Yet most informed Europeans residing in China felt that despite some misgivings about his overreliance on Moscow, Mao benefited from close association with Russia. Sweden's ambassador to China, Erik Boheman, believed that new Chinese war materiel and industrial equipment, however small in quantity, came almost solely from the Soviet Union and its East European clients and were fully appreciated by the recipients. As for a possible Chinese break from the Soviet Union, it was generally conceded in the State Department that "the Soviets have thought up ways for eliminating any Tito who may arise in China, also of blotting out Chou En-lai or any other Chinese Communist leader who might show inclination to repeat Chiang Kai-shek's performance."[17]

In the meantime, British and American leaders disagreed sharply on Western policy toward China. The Americans argued that London's recognition of China was both unwise and a failure because it was unreciprocated and had not borne anything important in Korea. Acheson further insisted, as did Dulles later, that the British should join willingly with the United States in pressing China hard on the battlefield and help punish China if it pushed aggression into other areas of Asia. And by all means, Acheson told Churchill during 1952 Anglo-American meetings, the British absolutely should discontinue trade and other economic relations with China. The courtship of Peking by the West, argued Acheson, was a dead issue, and further indulgence could serve no useful purpose. Although he admitted that some friction irritated the Russian-Chinese partnership and it was likely to get worse, he no longer believed that the West would very soon directly benefit. He maintained that

16. Office of Intelligence Research, Department of State, "Communist China: Satellite or Junior Partner of the USSR?" January 11, 1952, *Declassified Documents Quarterly*, IV (July-September, 1978), 263; Bruce to secretary of state, January 19, 1952, #793.11/1-1952, RG 59, NA; Clubb, memorandum of conversation, April 16, 1951, #793.11/4-1651, *ibid.*

17. Bland Calder, memorandum, May 24, 1951, #793.00/5-2451, RG 59, NA.

Chinese intervention in Korea created obstacles to any imminent reorientation by Peking away from Moscow, and concessions to China could not favorably modify CCP attitudes toward the West. Therefore, Acheson was determined that the United States and its allies force China hard militarily,
squeeze it economically, isolate it diplomatically, and make the going as tough
as possible for Mao, his colleagues, and the Kremlin.[18] Churchill's government, however, was never fully convinced of the soundness of American policy and protested that it merely reduced Western diplomatic maneuverability.

INDOCHINA

American policy in Indochina before and immediately after the Korean War
reveals changing U.S. perceptions of the Sino-Soviet alliance and the nature
of communist activity in Southeast Asia. In effect, the war caused the United
States to substitute China for Russia as the major enemy to Western interests
in Southeast Asia.

From 1946 through 1949, the administration regarded suppression of the
Viet Minh and France's attempts to establish a national puppet government
under Bao Dai merely as a local French problem. As the colonial war continued and Ho Chi Minh's resistance stiffened, the United States became increasingly concerned lest France's strength, needed in Europe against Russia, become severely drained. Respecting French attempts to encourage a
nationalist alternative to Ho, a writer of the *Pentagon Papers* observed, "It
is clear that American policymakers perceived the vacuity of French policies
in 1946 and 1947. The U.S., in its representations to France, consistently de-
plored the prospect of protracted war in Vietnam, and urged meaningful
concessions to Vietnamese nationalism."[19]

President Truman steadfastly refused to endorse Ho as the legitimate leader
of Vietnam's national movement because of his communist allegiance. (Ho
was, incidentally, a founding member of the French Communist party.) The
State Department believed at different times that Ho was a potential Tito-type
figure, but this understanding eventually was superseded by the knowledge
that his insurgency objectively served Soviet purposes. In late January, 1950,
shortly after the Soviet Union officially recognized Ho Chi Minh's Democratic Republic of Vietnam, Acheson stated that recognition by the Kremlin

18. Truman-Churchill Talks, January 7, 9, 1952, Acheson Papers; Steering Group Paper on
Preparations for Talks between the President and Prime Minister, January 5, 1952, *Declassified
Documents Quarterly*, VII (January–March, 1981), 96.
19. *The Pentagon Papers* (Gravel Edition, 4 vols., Boston, 1971), I, 28.

of Ho's communist movement removed any illusions about the "nationalist nature of his aims and reveals Ho in his true colors as the mortal enemy of native independence in Indochina." Still, Charles Yost of the Office of East European Affairs was not persuaded and wondered if Soviet recognition of Ho, which followed almost immediately after China's, indicated a Sino-Soviet contest for command in Indochina. If so, he ventured, this boded well both for the creation of hard feeling between Peking and Moscow and the eventual development of Titoism in China.[20] Yost, though, was overruled.

Gradually, the administration came to accept the so-called Bao Dai solution, despite serious doubts about his political effectiveness and limited popular appeal, and recognized his government in February, 1950. Skepticism about French possibilities for success aside, Truman supported his ally in recovering something of its prewar political eminence in Indochina. As early as 1946, the United States had granted France a $160 million credit for purchasing vehicles and military equipment for deployment in Indochina, but with communist victory in China and the advent of fighting in Korea came dramatically increased American involvement in Vietnam.

In response to an anticipated surge of communist activity along the Sino-Indochina border, the administration appropriated a few million dollars for military aid to Bao Dai's government in May, 1950. Ten million dollars more were granted to the entire Indochina area. Shortly thereafter, general hostilities in Korea led Truman to direct a dramatic acceleration in the supply of military assistance to French forces in Indochina.

After Chinese intervention in Korea, the administration feared China might follow suit in Southeast Asia. The NSC staff observed that "the danger of an overt military attack against Southeast Asia is inherent in the existence of a hostile and aggressive Communist China."[21] The defection of Southeast Asia to communism would imperil the rest of Asia, eventually Europe, and perhaps even ultimately the United States; the loss of any single country in Southeast Asia would have repercussions far beyond that area alone. Like a row of dominoes, the free world would collapse in Asia, and the West would suffer severe economic and diplomatic setbacks.

These inflated fears of geopolitical and psychological reverses were fully shared by the Joint Chiefs of Staff. In addition, they worried that Southeast Asian food supplies, once in communist hands, would adversely affect the

20. *Ibid.*, 41; John Gaddis, "Defense Perimeter Concept," in Borg and Heinrichs (eds.) *Uncertain Years*, 97.
21. NSC 124/2, June, 1952, NSC File, Modern Military Branch, NA.

overall Soviet-U.S. power balance. It was also noted in Washington at the time of China's successes in Korea that Chinese nationals in Southeast Asia warmly praised Peking and might cooperate in any campaigns waged against French Indochina.[22] In view of this perceived threat, the administration prepared detailed plans in 1951 to foil Chinese actions against Indochina.

In case of emergency, Truman and Acheson were willing to bomb mainland targets and impose a naval blockade along China's entire coast. Although such actions might lead to general hostilities between China and the United States, it was judged that Kremlin leaders would respond cautiously and do what they could to avoid direct Soviet involvement. The Chinese could expect Russian military supplies, but no more; only under extreme provocation would the Soviet armed forces engage American troops and air force: "We believe that the USSR will be less likely to make war over China [if] Western powers refrain from the conduct of operations against China in areas proximate to the USSR."[23]

After the Korean fighting ended, Eisenhower's administration anticipated that China would direct considerable attention to Indochina. On September 2, 1953, Secretary Dulles exclaimed, "Communist China has been and now is training, equipping and supplying the Communist forces in Indochina. There is the risk that, as in Korea, Red China might send its own army into Indochina. The Chinese Communist regime should realize that such a second aggression could not occur without grave consequences which might not be confined to Indochina."[24] Thus an incorrect understanding of China's essentially defensive intervention in Korea persisted, and the poorly learned lesson was misapplied to Indochina.

Throughout the Korean War, the United States was loath to consider using American troops in Indochina or to relieve French authorities of their responsibility for defending the Associated States. By late 1953, however, the United States had provided economic and military assistance to Indochina valued at $785 million. Unfortunately, by concentrating on the alleged threat posed by China, the United States inadvertently failed to encourage fully and support enthusiastically the fledgling noncommunist governments of Indochina. The central concern was to prevent aggression from the north, not to construct a resilient economic and political infrastructure. The United States was also re-

22. *FRUS, 1952–1954*, XIII (Part 1), 154.
23. Perkins, memorandum to Livingston Merchant, August 1, 1951, #793.00/8–151, RG 59, NA.
24. *Pentagon Papers*, I, 85–86.

luctant to push France strongly enough on taking measures to satisfy Vietnamese nationalism; simply put, Washington's overriding concern was to halt a potential Chinese-inspired communist conquest of Southeast Asia.[25] This priority in turn led Dulles, at the Geneva Conference in 1954, to attempt to rescue French prestige and preserve for the West something of a foothold in Indochina, but the United States never found a national, popular alternative to the communist Ho Chi Minh.

TRANSITIONS, 1953

The new Republican administration that came to office in early 1953 immediately assumed a militant public stand against communism and employed the provocative rhetoric of "rollback" and "liberation." Beneath stylistic changes, however, the Republicans soon demonstrated that they would retain the substance of Truman's foreign policy. Status quo defense, not revision of East-West divisions in Europe, marked the foreign policy of Dulles and Eisenhower. For example, in June, 1953—five months after Eisenhower's inauguration—when Soviet tanks subdued a workers' spontaneous rebellion in East Berlin, the American government merely sent ineffectual protests to the United Nations and encouraged passive German resistance. Despite a superiority in nuclear weapons, the prudent Americans exercised restraint and in effect acknowledged the sanctity of a Soviet sphere of influence in central and Eastern Europe.

The administration's official rhetoric was largely a result of campaign propaganda, the momentum of which forced expression in formal policy pronouncements. During the 1952 campaign, Dulles had preached the immorality of mere containment and the folly of appeasing tyrannical communism. Large numbers of voters were persuaded that a Republican administration would defiantly oppose communism (unlike the spineless Democrats, many of whom were sympathetic to Moscow anyway) and win back for the West the miserable peoples of Soviet-controlled Eastern Europe. Rollback, though, was never a realistic alternative. Once safely installed in the White House, Eisenhower confronted the same grim realities as his predecessor; exaggerated campaign speeches did not mitigate the horrors of a Soviet-American thermonuclear exchange. Nevertheless, a firm public stand against communism assured voters and Kremlin leaders alike of American "resolve." Improved relations with China were virtually impossible for any American ad-

25. *Ibid.*, 87.

ministration in the early 1950s, particularly for one whose political life relied on conservative backers violently opposed to rapprochement with Red China. Eisenhower himself regretted that the domestic political situation was so inconducive to flexible policy toward the People's Republic.[26]

The relationship between the new chief Republican policy makers, Dulles and Eisenhower, was marked after some initial awkwardness by trust and mutual respect. According to standard scholarship, the president, less well versed and less experienced in the intricacies of international affairs, usually deferred to Dulles; consequently, he built one of the most powerful secretaryships in recent times and beyond doubt was the responsible architect for Republican foreign policy. Yet in recent years, President Eisenhower has enjoyed greater respect from scholars, who assert that not only did he occasionally lapse into periods of lucidity but was supremely confident in his judgments on foreign problems, was extremely able, and had benefited from years of wartime cooperation with European civilian and military leaders. Referring to Dulles, the president once reportedly admitted, "There's only one man I know who has seen more of the world and talked with more people and knows more than he does—and that's me." One diplomatic historian has written that Eisenhower chose Dulles because he was knowledgeable and a seasoned diplomat but would yield to the president.[27] Nevertheless, Dulles was particularly competent with regard to the Far East, and most evidence suggests that the president relied heavily on his expertise and advice.

Dulles had become especially prominent in international policy work as a consultant to Secretary of State Acheson. Dulles' appointment in 1950 was part of Truman's strategy to preserve bipartisanship in diplomacy, which at the time was rapidly eroding under Republican and McCarthyite attacks. At first grateful for his intelligent, hard work on the Japanese Peace Treaty, Acheson eventually came to despise his successor. The normally gracious and courtly Acheson perceived Dulles as uncommonly ambitious and as a groveler before McCarthy and his creatures. Indeed, throughout his tenure as secretary, Dulles was extremely touchy about aspersions against his integrity from the political right. As chairman of the Carnegie Endowment Board, Dulles had in 1946 recommended Alger Hiss for president of the Carnegie Endowment for International Peace. Four years later, notorious Freda Utely, in testimony before Senator Tydings' investigating committee, implicated Dulles

26. Memorandum, "Discussion at the 271st meeting of the NSC," December 23, 1955, Eisenhower Papers (Whitman File).

27. Robert Divine, *Eisenhower and the Cold War Years* (Oxford, 1981), 21–22.

in Hiss's alleged misdeeds. Dulles promptly responded with a rush of correspondence to Tydings and was quickly cleared of any suspicion; the episode was most unpleasant for Dulles, however, and may account for the timidity with which he later approached McCarthy, even at the expense of such subordinates as John Paton Davies, John Service, and Charles Bohlen.

In any case, the conventional liberal view of Dulles—that he had the gravity of Solomon but none of his wisdom—is exaggerated. To his contemporaries, Dulles was an infinitely complicated, sophisticated man. Sherman Adams, White House assistant to Eisenhower, admired Dulles as a stark realist. Robert Bowie, State Department member of Eisenhower's NSC, believed Dulles was a flexible man whose subtle understanding of international affairs sharply contrasted with his simple black-white public pronouncements. According to George Kennan, never charitable to dullards and hardly beholden to Dulles, Eisenhower's secretary was a cold, ambitious figure, probably not God-fearing at all. Yet Kennan claims that though Dulles never admitted it, he was wise enough to take as inspiration Kennan's precepts on international relations. And Eisenhower, despite some early misgivings about Dulles—related in part to Dulles' enthusiastic advocacy of a "liberation policy" during the presidential campaign, never a dear or practical project to the general—soon came to respect his secretary and increasingly looked to him for advice and guidance. Eisenhower once recorded in his diary, "There is probably no one in the world who has the technical competence of Foster Dulles in the diplomatic field. He has spent his life in this work in one form or another and is a man of great intellectual capacity and moral courage." Robert Divine, a contemporary historian, claims that Dulles' "moralistic and often ponderous public statements gave him the reputation, which he cherished, of being a dedicated crusader against the Soviets; behind the scenes he proved to have a lucid understanding of the realities of world politics and a surprising gift for the give-and-take of diplomacy."[28] Whatever the essential truth about Dulles, who was surely as enigmatic as he was formidable, his views and those of his staff about a number of foreign policy subjects, including the nature of international communism, were hardly altogether primitive.

Less than two months after assuming office, the administration noted events in Moscow that augured well for a Cold War thaw. Stalin's successors, seemingly moderate men, were preoccupied with consolidating their power, not

28. Sherman Adams, Dulles Oral History Project, p. 15; Robert Bowie, *ibid.*, pp. 42–47; George Kennan, *ibid.*, pp. 39–45; Mudd Library, Princeton University, Princeton, N.J.; Robert Ferrell (ed.), *The Eisenhower Diaries* (New York, 1981), 306; Divine, *Eisenhower*, 22.

with causing problems for the West. Even so, the Soviet Union probably would have initiated moves toward the West even if the Genius Leader of Progressive Mankind had not died in March, 1953. Only a few months before his death, Stalin had issued an essay at the Nineteenth Party Congress titled "Economic Problems of Socialism," in which prospects for peaceful coexistence were discussed. In the West, though, Stalin was largely held responsible for the Cold War, and his passing provided the Kremlin with an opportunity to improve East-West relations.

The major goal of his successor, Georgi Malenkov, was to avoid a Soviet-American military conflict. After all, war against the most powerful state could only produce catastrophe for the Socialist Fatherland; secondary concerns also indicated the desirability of easing global tensions. Soviet military and industrial programs were expensive and had to be curtailed, freeing resources for traditionally neglected domestic programs. Though long accustomed to self-sacrifice, the Soviet people hoped for an improved standard of living. And that perennial Russian nemesis, unreliable agricultural production, required more attention. Improved relations with the West could also lead to negotiations toward a definitive German settlement, understandably critical to Moscow, and could mean increased trade with the technologically advanced Americans and West Europeans. Infusions of Western technology into the relatively backward Soviet economy would doubtless boost capital and consumer goods production. The Soviet leadership's diplomatic, political, and economic preoccupations were implicit in Malenkov's concluding remarks to the Supreme Soviet in August, 1953: "We stand, as we have always stood, for the peaceful co-existence of the two systems. We hold there are no objective reasons for clashes between the United States of America and the Soviet Union. The security of the two states and of the world, and the development of trade between the United States of America and the Soviet Union, can be assured on the basis of normal relations between the two countries."[29]

In 1954, political rivalry within the collective leadership gave rise to a policy dispute about the wisdom of stressing consumer goods over heavy industry and resulted in Malenkov's forced resignation in February, 1955. (CIA analysts speculated at the time that Malenkov might have been pushed aside by other members of the collective leadership because he failed to support China adequately in both its modernization drive and its trials against America.) In any event, the need to alleviate Soviet-American tensions for the sake

29. R. V. Daniels, *A Documentary History of Communism* (2 vols., New York, 1960), II, 217.

of attending to domestic problems remained a constant motive in the Soviet pursuit of increased international stability. Gradually, a convergence of interest, rooted in mutual fear and reinforced by Soviet internal requirements, formed the basis of limited Soviet-American cooperation, which from a Soviet point of view was necessarily pursued at the expense of China.

Beginning in late 1953, Chinese emulation of Stalinist modernization, embodied in the slogan "Learn from the Soviet Union," was curtailed in favor of Maoist innovations. These included experiments with mutual aid teams, collective management of communes, raising of the countryside's economic and political status, and decentralization of the control and production of Chinese industry. Chinese modification of Marxist "scientific development" amounted to a qualification of Soviet experience as universal and dignified independent socialist initiative.

Moscow's communist leadership was also compromised during the post-Stalin succession struggle. Both Khrushchev and Malenkov sought legitimacy by claiming for themselves close friendship and understanding with Mao. By invoking Peking's prestige and authority, rival Soviet fractions undoubtedly strengthened Mao's inclination to see himself as heir to the Marx-Lenin-Stalin apostolic succession. The British embassy in Peking reported to Dulles that the Chinese May Day celebration in 1953 prominently featured Mao's image, while Malenkov's was rarely seen and was far surpassed by pictures of Stalin. Moreover, the Kremlin leadership squabble very likely enabled Mao to eliminate a Soviet-backed rival, Kao Kang, who had established for himself a semiautonomous fief in Manchuria, where the great bulk of Soviet industrial aid to China had been concentrated. One of the important charges against Kao in 1954 was that he worked as an agent for a foreign power; his purge meant removal of an irritating Russian influence in the CCP and allowed Peking to exert total authority over the important border province. (State Department analysts speculated shortly afterward that Kao's fall was related to his inability to deliver Soviet goods on a scale commensurate with Peking's needs.) [30] Concatenate with problems of Chinese development and mutual domestic meddling—recalled by both sides only much later—were diverging security interests and the issue of Soviet commitment to Chinese rebuilding programs.

30. Tomlinson to Johnson, May 5, 1953, #793.00/5–553, RG 59, NA; Office of Intelligence Research, Department of State, "Asian Communist Orbit 1955," January, 1956, *Declassified Documents Quarterly*, II (July–September, 1976), 173.

AMERICAN PERCEPTIONS OF THE SINO-SOVIET ALLIANCE, 1953

The CIA believed that the initial impact of Stalin's death on Sino-Soviet cooperation was slight. Yet the CIA also doubted that any successor to Stalin would have prestige in Asia comparable to his: "The stature of Mao as leader and theoretician of Asian Communism will inevitably increase with the disappearance of the former supreme leader. Mao will almost certainly have more influence in the determination of Bloc policy affecting Asia." Although the CIA believed Mao would not seek leadership of the international communist movement, Moscow would probably deal very cautiously with him. Otherwise, "serious strains in Sino-Soviet relations will almost certainly develop."[31]

The new administration had some evidence of Sino-Soviet tensions that, if not promising severe discord between the two powers, at least offered reason to hope. A case in point was the autumn 1952 Sino-Soviet meetings, which revealed ample evidence of difficulties: Soviet promises to relinquish privileges in Manchuria and Port Arthur were unredeemed, and Russian military and economic aid to China was not increased substantially. According to General Walter Bedell Smith, director of central intelligence, the inadequate Soviet help was not a coincidence but was perfectly predictable. Shortly before the Sino-Soviet conference, he commented, "The Chinese are obviously coming to Moscow to ask for more help because they are losing a great deal of material and energy in Korea. The Russians will drive a hard price. At all costs they do not intend to see built up on their eastern frontier a Chinese military Frankenstein monster."[32]

During early 1953, American broadcasts to China, aimed at stirring popular unrest with the regime and exciting Peking's impatience with Moscow, stressed the disastrous effects for China of dependence on the Soviet Union. Moscow's return of the Changchun Railway to Peking, for example, was ridiculed by the Voice of America for granting China only "paper control of its transportation." VOA celebrated the third anniversary of formal Russian-Chinese alliance with an imaginary Chinese citizen-on-the-street, who reported that the Peking-Moscow observance day festival was "nice." "It ought to be. It was very expensive. We paid with Port Arthur, the Changchun Railway, Sinkiang and—let's see—the war in Korea." Also, according to VOA, China's economic rehabilitation was very slow, thanks to "underwhelming"

31. CIA Special Estimate, "Probable Consequences of the Death of Stalin and the Elevation of Malenkov to Leadership in the USSR," March 10, 1953, Jackson Papers.
32. C. L. Sulzberger, *A Long Row of Candles* (Toronto, 1969), 778–79.

Soviet aid. Even so, Chinese soldiers were useful cannon fodder in Moscow's imperialist adventures.[33]

Stalin's death also inspired themes for American propagandists. VOA reporters wondered whether Mao would continue to obey Moscow, now under a revolutionary novice, Malenkov, and whether China would still mindlessly fetch and serve as a Soviet lackey in foreign policy. One broadcast ended with the words "Will Mao allow himself to be again humiliated? Is the Communist regime's grip on the Chinese people strong enough to survive another era of Soviet contempt for and exploitation of China?"[34]

In addition, Stalin's death provided an unusual opportunity for the "imaginative" handling of covert operations. Harold Stassen, director of the Mutual Security and Psychological Strategy Board, arranged to send an American newspaper publisher to Peking to interview Mao. Stassen believed the journalist's "attempts to get to see Mao will cause uneasiness in both the USSR and China, and if he does see him, it will increase suspicions in every respect."[35] Rumors and speculations were also planted among Western commentators and writers that Malenkov had a hit-list and Mao was the first to be liquidated. In this context VOA broadcast a report titled "Whose Funeral Is Next?"

Meanwhile, Sino-Soviet problems entirely unrelated to American machinations were evident to CIA analysts. In a September, 1953, report covering the period 1949–1952, they examined Mao's theoretical corpus in relation to its relevance (and China's) to colonial struggles and predicted that a deterioration in relations between Peking and Moscow would first be signaled by divergent assertions regarding theoretical matters. The CIA report further observed that Soviet critiques of Mao's written works, while praising him, were careful to avoid attributions of originality; these were reserved only for Lenin and Stalin. To have made such claims, argued intelligence analysts, would have meant promoting Mao to an unacceptably high position of esteem. Its ideological supremacy indirectly challenged, Moscow's socialist leadership would be jeopardized. Soviet reviewers therefore insisted on referring to Marx, Engels, Lenin, and Stalin as the important contributors to communist theory; Mao's work, albeit worthy, was essentially derivative and depended on Lenin's and especially Stalin's pioneering. Similar appraisals were made of Mao

33. Voice of America, "Ceremony at Harbin," January 7, 1953; ibid., "Friendship Treaty Bargain Rates," February 13, 1954; ibid., [title illegible], February 16, 1953. VOA manuscripts, University of California Library, Berkeley, Calif.

34. Ibid., "Time for Decisions in China," March 6, 1953.

35. Harold Stassen, memorandum, "Stalin's Death," March 10, 1953, Jackson Papers.

as a military tactician, who had skillfully and faithfully applied Lenin's and Stalin's ideas during the Chinese civil war.

Not fully appreciated abroad, the master was revered at home. Shen Chih-yuan remarked that "Chairman Mao is indubitably the world's most outstanding teacher of creative Marxism-Leninism since Lenin and Stalin"; Chou En-lai expressed similar sentiments. According to the CIA's September analysis, Chinese critics originally implied, and later explicitly proclaimed, that China's revolution—not Russia's—was pertinent to other Asian revolutionary struggles. One Chinese apologist was quoted as predicting, "China's revolution today . . . is the tomorrow of Vietnam, Burma, Ceylon, India and the other various Asian colonial and semi-colonial nations."[36]

Earnest Soviet ideologues were neither convinced nor amused. The analysts noted that in late 1951 all Chinese discussions of "Mao's road" and China as revolutionary exemplar ceased, presumably the victim of Soviet censorship; Mao, in effect, was forced to retract exalted claims that he was an outstanding, creative Marxist-Leninist theorist. That November at a conference of the Soviet Oriental Institute, the principal speaker, Ye Zhukov, explained, "It would be risky to regard the Chinese revolution as some kind of 'stereotype' for people's democratic revolutions in other countries of Asia"; rather, Lenin, Stalin, and Soviet experience were the progenitors of true doctrine applicable in the East. The CIA reporters wrote that the Chinese accepted these pronouncements only after a delay and even then unwillingly. "It would be surprising if the Chinese Communist elite had not been disturbed by these conclusions. The consequent decline in prestige for China's revolution and for its theoretician, Mao Tse-tung, was unmistakable." The report concluded cautiously that ideological and political problems between China and the Soviets were latent, though full of possibility. Eventually, the Chinese might rebel. But for the time being, China's industrialization program depended on Soviet aid, and thus Moscow's influence in Peking was considerable; Mao was having "a sufficiently difficult task in the consolidation and stabilization of China's economy and can look to few other countries for assistance."[37]

If the CIA authors of the quotations above meant to imply that America might still use its economic might to lure China away from the Soviet Union, they were not alone among observers urging such a line. Earlier in the year, retired Admiral Ellis Zacharias had advised Sherman Adams, "Today, China

36. Philip Bridgham, Arthur Cohen, and Leonard Jaffe, "Mao's Road and Sino-Soviet Relations: A View from Washington, 1953," *China Quarterly*, LII (October–December 1972), 682.
37. *Ibid.*, 670–98.

is offered no realistic alternative to her present orientation. An operation plan to provide such an alternative, without appeasement, but with a realistic and positive approach, is both feasible and vital. Such a plan should not be discussed openly, but it has been formulated in detail.'' Only a couple of weeks after Zacharias sent his letter, Charlton Ogburn, an adviser for the State Department's Bureau of Far Eastern Affairs, complained to his superiors that the only rational policy toward China was to detach it from the Soviet camp, but so far American actions were merely encouraging Chinese reliance on Moscow. He suggested emphatically that the entire China policy of the United States ought to be overhauled in the direction of recognition, UN admission, and restored trade relations.[38]

Yet in 1953 the government was hardly in a position to take advantage of these recommendations; to pursue a policy even remotely smacking of conciliation with Mao would have been tantamount to challenging McCarthy, something that neither the administration nor most members of Congress were willing to do. In addition, an inflexible anticommunist pose helped reassure Taiwan. A case in point occurred during Dulles' confirmation hearings, when he stated that if People's China declared itself independent of Russia, it might then be advisable for the United States to seek normal relations with the government in Peking. This statement led H. P. Tseng, director of Taiwan's Central News Agency, to argue passionately that Red China could never throw off Russia's control.

Ambassador Rankin later explained, ''Among the most disturbing and unacceptable ideas to the leaders of Free China is the suggestion that 'Titoism' might appear in Red China or that, through some other development, the communist regimes in Moscow and Peiping might cleave asunder.'' He maintained that many Chinese on Taiwan believed Mao actually enjoyed a high degree of independence from Moscow, and they worried that if the United States should accept this notion as true, it would then follow the lead of Britain and India and adopt a more generous policy toward the People's Republic: ''Only so long as they are persuaded that Americans continue to regard Mao simply as a Soviet tool will they [the Nationalists] feel reasonably assured as to our policy.'' In fact, as early as 1949, Chiang had tried to disabuse Western observers of ''insidious,'' ''false'' speculation that Mao would imitate Tito's defiance.[39]

38. Zacharias to Sherman Adams, May 9, 1953, OF 8-c/18-d (1), Eisenhower Library; *FRUS, 1952–1954*, III, 640.
    39. Rankin to secretary of state, January 30, 1953, #793.00/1-3053, RG 59, NA; Rankin, *China Assignment*, 173; *FRUS, 1949*, VIII, 412–13.

Still, the administration, especially Dulles, managed to perpetuate a clear-headed, pragmatic policy, but, from political and diplomatic necessity, one that was sheltered from public scrutiny. Notwithstanding Kennan's criticisms at the time of the proposed Korean armistice negotiations in 1950, Dulles, as a member of the Democratic administration and later as secretary of state, believed that the Soviets had a somewhat doubtful ally in China, and he favored harassing the communist alliance.[40] Certainly, splitting the communist powers was entirely consistent with his view of international politics. His rigid, moralistic rhetoric did not rule out the possibility that virtue and the Lord's work could be advanced by duping Lucifer's agents into confounding each other.

During a February, 1952, interview on "Meet the Press," Dulles stated that as a general proposition, "if your major objective is to get a break [between a given Marxist state and] Moscow, the way to get that is to make the going tough, not easy." He maintained that Tito broke from Moscow because Western resistance to Yugoslavia in Greece and the economic blockade caused severe problems for Belgrade, which the Soviets could not alleviate. Therefore, to check the spread of economic and social deterioration at home, the Yugoslavs sought an accommodation with the West at the expense of their connection with Moscow. Dulles claimed that the alliance between Moscow and Peking posed a "great danger" for the United States: "If we could break that, that would certainly be a great advantage." He then explained, "I would have a policy which is designed to make the going so tough for the present regime in China that it's going to change in some way." It might be changed from within; it might be changed by a radical shift away from Moscow: "The essential thing is to have action which will bring about a change."[41]

Later, during the height of the 1952 presidential campaign, Dulles publicly advocated "activating strains and stresses within the Russian Communist empire so as to disintegrate it." All of the East European satellite states and China should be split away from the Soviet Union, thereby depriving Moscow of valuable manpower pools, natural resources, and prestige. He was most revealing, however, in his discussion in mid-November, 1952, with George Yeh, Taipei's foreign minister, and Wellington Koo, Nationalist ambassador to Washington. Then secretary-designate, Dulles urged that Sino-Soviet bonds could be severed by "keeping [Communist China] under pressures which

40. See Dulles' memorandum for Acheson, November 30, 1950, Box 47, Dulles Papers, and Dulles-Bowles correspondence, April 23, May 1, 1952, Box 58, Dulles Papers.
41. Dulles interview on "Meet the Press," transcript, February 10, 1952, *ibid.*

would, in turn, keep the Communists pressuring Russia for more than Russia would give." Eventually, Dulles hoped, China could play an independent role in Far Eastern international affairs and contribute to a stable balance of power.[42]

Dulles' proposed handling of the Sino-Soviet alliance fitted logically into his general foreign policy. In effect, it emphasized the bludgeon—the Eisenhower administration's doctrine of massive retaliation, for example—over the rapier. Applied to the communist alliance, Dulles hoped it would menace or at least fatigue the allies apart. Diplomatic pressures against Peking should be combined with implied threats of instantaneous nuclear destruction of China and Russia if the former misbehaved. And in peacetime, Russia would risk overextending its limited financial and material resources; as much as possible, Moscow should bear alone the full weight of aiding impoverished China.

Republican policy during the waning months of Korean fighting was not essentially different from Truman's. The new National Security Council also hoped to encourage strains within the Sino-Soviet alliance through steadily applied pressure. Yet the NSC doubted that American actions could basically realign Peking's acceptance of Soviet leadership. Consequently, once the Korean War ended, the administration did not worry overmuch that sound diplomacy was impaired by continued aid to, and recognition of, Taiwan. American leaders seriously felt by the time of the Korean truce that in 1950 Russia had sabotaged Peking's admission to the United Nations. By mid-1953, however, most top administration officials doubted that China's admission would encourage Mao to cooperate with the West.[43]

Like its predecessor, the Eisenhower administration had difficulties in managing a united Western front. To Dulles' annoyance, both British and Greek traders resumed business in China immediately after the Korean War. The British were fully convinced that the Chinese leadership, desperate to diversify the economy and strengthen and modernize heavy industry, recognized that the Soviets—especially after Malenkov's call for new emphasis on consumer goods—were not to be relied upon; only the West could furnish

42. Dulles, Address to Chicago Council on Foreign Relations: "Containment Is Not the Only Alternative to War," October 8, 1952, Dulles Papers; Dulles' account of meeting with Bebler, the Yugoslav vice minister for foreign affairs, June 24, 1952, Dulles-Herter Papers, Eisenhower Library; Dulles, memorandum of conversation with George Yeh and Wellington Koo, November 14, 1952, Dulles Papers.

43. NSC 147, April 2, 1953, NSC File, Modern Military Branch, NA; *FRUS, 1952–1954*, III, 646–47. The NSC as constituted under Eisenhower included, in addition to himself, Vice-President Nixon, Secretary Dulles, Defense Secretary Charles Wilson, Harold Stassen of the Foreign Operations Administration, Arthur Fleming, director of defense mobilization, and Robert Cutler, national security adviser.

sufficient quantities of those items that China most sought. In the expectation of winning some political concessions (for example, over Hong Kong) or at least of not encouraging further Chinese dependence on Russia, Churchill's government therefore promoted better economic relations with Mao's regime.[44] After the armistice the prevailing view in London was that U.S. policy was notable only for Dulles' "elephantine obstinacy," which foolishly prolonged Sino-Soviet cooperation. The administration's careful review of policy toward China in autumn 1953 surely did nothing to relieve British bewilderment at their ally's bluster.

Similar to Truman's NSC, the newly constituted Republican council admitted in November, 1953, "The primary problem of U.S. foreign policy in the Far East is to cope with the altered structure of power which arises from the existence of a strong and hostile Communist China, and from the alliance of Communist China with the U.S.S.R."[45] Furthermore, reckoned the NSC, even if Far Eastern problems over Taiwan, Korea, and Indochina should be resolved to Peking's satisfaction, its hostility toward the West, especially the United States, would fester on.

Respecting the Sino-Soviet alliance, the NSC believed—despite intelligence analyses such as the one just considered—that "powerful ties of common ideology" secured the partnership. Coinciding national interests also bound the alliance, and its value to each state had recently been proven. China had obtained Soviet material and technical assistance to develop the armed forces, build extracting industries, establish power plants, and improve transportation facilities. The Russians also supported Chinese attempts to gain international acceptance and proclaimed Peking as a great power. Finally, the Soviet alliance provided China with immunity from direct American attack during the Korean War. In turn, Moscow profited from China's defense of Korea, which prevented installation of a hostile government along part of the Soviet frontier; Chinese propaganda also helped spread Soviet influence in the Far East. In short, their association effectively promoted the interests of each party, and "the conflicts of interest of both partners with the non-communist world are for the present much more intense than conflicts of interest between the partners."[46]

Immediate and long-term hazards, however, could rot Sino-Soviet friendship. These "potential dangers to the alliance will stem primarily from the

44. Zimmerman to secretary of state, September 4, 1953, #793.00/9–453, RG 59, NA.
45. NSC 166/1, November 6, 1953, NSC File, Modern Military Branch, NA.
46. *Ibid.*

inner workings of the partnership and only secondarily from the nature of external pressures or inducements.'' The primary dangers were rooted in Chinese nationalism, whose ambitions, embodied by the CCP, included international communist leadership and national goals incompatible with Soviet aims. Over the short term, Chinese desires to reassert sovereignty in Port Arthur might cause Russian irritation. Other specific, unresolved problems (such as Soviet intervention in Manchuria, Sinkiang, and Mongolia; Mao's undetermined status in world communism; CCP influence in South Asian and Japanese Communist parties; and Chinese repayment of Soviet military and economic aid) jeopardized the alliance. In addition, Chinese self-development was thought to vex the Russians. The Kremlin could ''hardly view with equanimity the development of an independent China on its frontiers which was powerful, well armed, industrially competent, and politically united. Chinese Communist successes in achieving reduction of Western power and influence in the Far East might confront the Russians with a partner whose ambitions could be achieved at cost not to the West but to the Russians themselves.'' Peking's military and industrial prowess might one day threaten Moscow's hold on Siberia.[47]

Although persuaded that external pressure alone could not break the alliance, the NSC declared, ''The West . . . can strive to create those pressures or inducements which might be most apt to provide the context for increase of tension in the partnership.''[48] To this object several policy options were considered. First, either alone or in conjunction with Taiwanese forces, the United States could on an appropriate occasion overthrow and replace the Peking regime. But the problems with such a policy were numerous. In the first place, America's European allies would probably balk and oppose such a

47. The NSC recorded: ''It may . . . become increasingly difficult for the Russians to maintain the circumspection which they have hitherto displayed in dealing with the sensibilities of their junior partner. The men of the Kremlin are not in the habit of dealing with their lessers in any terms except those of strict control. New strains within the Kremlin leadership might prompt the Chinese communists, confident of their own regime's stability, to adopt an attitude of arrogance and greater independence. As the inevitable differences in interest, viewpoint, or timing of actions develop between the Russians and the Chinese; as the Chinese tend to become importunate in their demands for Russian assistance or support; or as the role of the Chinese as viceregents for international communism in the Far East becomes too independent and self reliant—there will be strong temptation for the Russians to attempt to move in the direction of greater disciplinary control over the Chinese Communists. If the time ever comes when the Russians feel impelled to contest with the Chinese Communist leaders for primacy in the domestic apparatus of control of the Chinese regime, the alliance will be critically endangered. For, as has been stated before, the Chinese Communist leaders are Chinese as well as Communists'' (NSC 166/1, November 6, 1953, NSC File, Modern Military Branch, NA).
48. Ibid.

venture. And should general war result, China could at least expect considerable Soviet military aid, while for the United States war would exact large costs in mobilization, inflict high casualties, and divert forces from Europe. Global war would be risked; atomic weapons might be used. Obviously, the dangers of such a policy were too great.

Another possibility was to offer China concessions designed to overcome its hostility and distrust. Perhaps agreements favorable to Peking could be reached on Taiwan's disposition, UN forces in Korea, and France's struggle to recover Indochina. This policy, too, was rejected on the grounds that America's security position would seriously weaken if Taiwan reverted to mainland control and Western forces withdrew from areas contiguous to China. It was feared that Peking's influence would fill the void, and "free Asia" would soon capitulate. Besides, concessions could not ease Chinese ideological antagonism toward the West nor necessarily provide incentive to loosen ties with Moscow.

Despite limited capabilities for increasing pressures inside China, the NSC decided to seek through continued economic restrictions to delay and make more difficult "Chinese Communist efforts to achieve industrialization and oblige the USSR to continue to carry the burden of assisting Communist China." Simultaneously, through various political measures, the United States should seek to impede universal acceptance of Peking and reduce its propaganda value for the Soviets. The United States would, meanwhile, continue to buttress the political, economic, and military strength of noncommunist Asian countries. The NSC planned to refortify offshore island security, check any Chinese expansion—with American forces if necessary—assist in anti-subversion programs of friendly states, establish a regional collective security system, and aid Taiwan and Japan in all important matters.[49] The administration also remained ever alert to any Sino-Soviet problems accessible to American diplomacy and was especially confident that stiff Soviet-Chinese competition over Sinkiang, the Mongolian Republic, and Manchuria would eventually develop; therein lay the seeds of future conflict.

By December, 1953, it had become acutely evident to British and American leaders that their approaches to China remained at odds and that in the interests of allied cooperation these differences should be reconciled. Consequently, when French, British, and U.S. heads of state met in Bermuda in early December, one of the issues they discussed was Western policy toward

49. NSC 166/1 was the single most comprehensive assessment made of American policy toward China during Eisenhower's first administration.

China. The assessment of Sino-Soviet relations given by Dulles to the assembled leaders was reasonable enough, but it did not meet with general approval; both Churchill and Anthony Eden withheld their assent.

The secretary explained to his British colleagues that, although he could not be entirely confident about the real nature of Sino-Soviet relations, he suspected that the communist alliance was becoming more tenuous. After all, Mao was an outstanding communist leader in his own right, whose prestige, though less than Stalin's, far outstripped Malenkov's. It was very likely, reasoned Dulles, that Mao would no longer be content to play a role subordinate to the Soviets. Probably Soviet eulogizing of Mao was prompted by the need to treat him as an equal partner and an important world leader. Dulles punctuated his remarks with optimism when he asserted that ever-competitive Sino-Soviet relations held the promise of a future Russian-Chinese break.

He next contrasted British and American approaches to China. Dulles doubted that British attempts at "being nice to the Communist Chinese" could succeed in weaning them from the Soviets. Yet American tactics relying on maximum pressure toward China could produce tangible strains in the alliance. Russia would simply not be able to meet Chinese demands, and the alliance's inevitable deterioration would speed along. Short of war, Dulles argued that the United States should concentrate its economic, political, and military strength against China. If America's allies joined this policy, it was probable that intracommunist problems would develop all the sooner; but Britain's policy would only lead to a dead end. And if the United Kingdom's approach should be adopted by others, China would soon enjoy the best of all worlds as Russia and the West competed for its favor. Dulles warned, moreover, that contradictory Western policies toward China impaired progress and enabled the communist states to exploit Western differences. He naturally did not expect Great Britain to withdraw its recognition of China; British leaders, he regretfully allowed, believed "one must recognize even one's enemies." Even so, political, economic, and moral aid did not follow automatically from recognition. Dulles hoped very much that Britain would join America in thwarting China's UN admission and would in other ways coordinate its policy with Washington against China.[50]

Foreign Minister Eden, diffident but unimpressed by the secretary's analysis, agreed that allied actions could help undermine Sino-Soviet cooperation. He also stated his belief that the communist leaders were intent on spoil-

50. *FRUS, 1952–1954*, III, 711–13.

ing Anglo-French-American unity. And yet, that in itself was not a reason to break all contacts with Peking, no matter how unsatisfactory London's "relationship with the Chinese Communists might be at present."[51]

Following Eden's slim rebuttal, the meeting adjourned without Anglo-American agreement. Once again, the policy of London and Washington toward the communist alliance was unsuccessfully resolved to the consternation of both governments.

Despite the failure of the United States to divide China from the Soviet Union, which culminated in Sino-American fighting in Korea, the notion persisted in Washington that security interests in the Far East would be served if Russian-Chinese friendship were diminished. General security in Western Europe might also be furthered. Chester Bowles, America's representative to India, declared: "With an uncertain China on its Pacific flank the Soviet Union would surely be forced to abandon its present policies of naked threats . . . in Europe and the Middle East and adopt some less explosive tactics." And though Dulles and other members of the NSC doubted that American actions could be decisive, they were anxious that the United States do what it could to break "the tie-up between Communist China and Moscow." This task was critical to the Eisenhower administration, just as it had been to Truman's.[52]

Complicating matters, the diplomacy of several European allies, but most importantly Great Britain, diverged from America's China policy and—complained Dulles—reduced the full economic and political pressure that the United States could concentrate against Peking. Still, Dulles had to face the unacceptable possibility that if he insisted too strongly to European governments that they follow America's lead against China, divisiveness would break out and perhaps cripple the Western coalition.[53]

51. *Ibid.*, 712–13.
52. Chester Bowles to Dulles, February 5, 1953, *Declassified Documents Quarterly*, V (April–June, 1979), 184.
53. NSC 5292, August, 1954; NSC 5429/1, December, 1954, NSC File, Modern Military Branch, NA.

Chapter V

FROM THE GENEVA CONFERENCES TO AMERICA'S REBUFF OF CHINA

Early in 1954, W. W. Rostow was completing work on his book *The Dynamics of Chinese Communist Society*. He was also in close touch with the CIA. In a report to the agency based on his recent research, Rostow argued that the Sino-Soviet alliance was "not intrinsically popular" in China. Suspicion among the informed Chinese public ran high that the "Big-brother relationship" was degenerating into a "Father-son relationship." Rostow believed that skillful, covert handling of Chinese apprehensions could increase general discontent with the CCP as well as cause problems for Moscow. He counseled that propaganda and rumors targeted against the "literate class" should emphasize various themes: Soviet advisers were progressively taking control of the Chinese government; food shortages in urban areas were attributable to exports to Russia and to high salaries paid Soviet advisers; and the Soviet Union was itself weak and therefore unreliable. It was coincidentally precisely this last point, the questionable value to China of Soviet friendship—and the dangers to Russia of supporting China—that the United States sought to impress upon communist leaders in 1954 and 1955.[1]

Walter Robertson, the assistant secretary of state for Far Eastern affairs, wrote in a letter in March, 1954: "It may be suspected that the last thing the

1. In the summer of 1952, several provinces in China were hard hit by crop failures caused by insect pests and abnormally late frost. Ten million people lived in the famine-stricken areas. Although the Chinese government allocated roughly 900,000 tons of food to relieve the desperate population, the government continued to export Manchurian wheat to Russia. American propagandists waxed eloquent on this episode and contrasted Soviet indifference during a period of crisis with American humanitarian programs to China between 1920 and 1950. W. W. Rostow to Franklin Lindsay, January 8, 1954, *Declassified Documents Quarterly*, V (January–March, 1979), 99.

Soviet Union desires is an aggressive and expansionist China—powerful in its own right—contiguous both to the Soviet Union's long Asian frontiers and to other Asian countries regarded as prizes by Moscow. If our refusal to contribute to the military power and prestige of the Peiping regime is for this reason a matter of delight to the Soviet Union, we may be confident that in time its delight will become apparent even to the Chinese Communists for all their ignorance and their fanatic misconceptions about the world."[2] As the following episodes illustrate, the United States was not altogether unsuccessful in helping Peking discover the true nature of Soviet ambition and concern regarding Chinese development and security.

GENEVA, 1954

In February, 1954, several months after the Korean armistice was signed, the foreign ministers of Britain, France, Russia, and the United States met in Berlin. Among other things, they scheduled a conference of all concerned parties, including Peking, to meet in the spring to resolve Korean-related issues and negotiate a settlement to the Indochina War. The Korean agenda at Geneva produced nothing. (Incidentally, when the conference commenced, Dulles wondered at Sino-Soviet competition for influence in North Korea and believed the Soviets feared that Mao wanted to absorb North Korea into Manchuria.[3]) Far-reaching, disastrous repercussions did spring from the sessions devoted to Indochina.

Congressional pressures directed at Dulles before the Geneva Conference were aimed at discouraging any intentions he may have entertained about meeting with Chou En-lai or improving Sino-American relations. As recently as November, 1953, Dulles had caused a stir in Taiwan and among Chiang's congressional supporters because of some apparently loose remarks. He seemed to imply that the American line toward China was softening and that if Peking should renounce aggression and quit taking orders from the Soviet Union, perhaps China would be eligible for American recognition and UN admission. Prompt "clarification" by Vice-President Richard Nixon of the secretary's comments helped put the matter to rest.

American conservatives, still not mollified, were vociferous in early 1954 for fear that contacts between the Chinese and American delegations might lead to America's recognition of Peking. In the words of Senator Herman

2. Robertson to Burton Young, March 22, 1954, Box 2861, RG 59, NA.
3. *FRUS, 1952–1954*, XVI, 16, 61.

Welker of Idaho, to do so would subvert that policy for which "American soldiers have paid in blood on the icy hills of Korea." Even the Berlin communiqué specifying the conditions of invitation to the Geneva Conference did not placate Senator Knowland. He found little comfort in assurances that "neither the invitation to nor the holding of the . . . conference shall be deemed to imply recognition in any case where it has not already been acceded." Rather, the senator from Formosa—as he was dubbed by the press—warned that the administration would be held accountable for any "slip" leading to recognition of the People's Republic or communist expansion in Indochina.[4] Facile parallels between Munich and Geneva were also drawn by various members of the Republican and Democratic parties.

Dulles' brief performance at the conference must have allayed all fears among China bloc congressmen. The secretary displayed singular diplomatic rudeness by refusing even to acknowledge the presence of Peking's delegation and wisecracked that he would not under any circumstances meet Chou En-lai, "unless our automobiles collide." Formal contact was never established between Chinese and American representatives during the conference's entire twelve weeks (April 26–July 21). As Dulles declared with characteristic earnestness, "It is one thing to recognize evil as a fact. It is another thing to take evil to one's breast and call it good." Meanwhile, of course, the Americans directly engaged their Soviet counterparts and informally met with Peking's delegates.[5]

Dulles' anticommunist policy at the minimum obviously distinguished gradations of Marxist acceptability. Indeed, Dulles and the administration might have gone very much further if it had not been for the inhibiting scorn of congressional critics. Toward the end of the Korean War, Eisenhower actually floated the idea that following a truce, China might rightfully enter the United Nations; though the president did not push the idea, it did at one point cause considerable domestic and international speculation.

Never convinced that prolonged nonrecognition of China served U.S. interests and doubtful about the long-term resilience of the Russian-Chinese alliance, Eisenhower also asked Churchill in June, 1954, if, under the right circumstances, he would use his good offices to help establish full, formal Sino-American relations. Sensibly impressed by Acheson's failure to retain public confidence, however, Dulles and Eisenhower acted cautiously and in-

4. *Congressional Record*, January 14, 1954, pp. 232–33.
5. Sulzberger, *Long Row of Candles*, 1003. Dulles, Speech to Overseas Press Club of America, March 29, 1954, Dulles Papers; *FRUS, 1952–1954*, XVI, 4.

directly when they tested the limits of right-wing tolerance. The experience of Arthur Dean, special ambassador to Korea and chief American delegate at Panmunjom, also revealed plenty to the president and his secretary.

Dean publicly suggested in early 1954 that Washington review its policy toward China; he resurrected the old idea that the United States could drive a wedge between China and Russia by improving relations with Mao's government. But Knowland, Welker, Judd, and others of their ilk found such an idea ludicrous. Welker, for example, countered that "the leaders of Communist China have, by their statements and their military actions, proved themselves to be complete tools of the international Communist conspiracy and its plan for world conquest." The senator ridiculed Dean's call for greater realism and asked rhetorically what was so unrealistic about America's China policy: "To me the refusal of a policy to offer the slightest concessions to the Red Chinese is the absolute height of realism. It is a real policy because it refuses to offer a bribe to the slave rulers of China . . . it refuses even to discuss the possibility of United Nations membership for a bloody aggressor whose policies have brought murderous ruin and destruction to millions."[6] Welker concluded by connecting Dean to a number of supposedly communist organizations, including the Institute of Pacific Relations, and purportedly unsavory characters such as Owen Lattimore. The charges were absurd, of course, but they reached a wide audience and clung like a straitjacket around the diplomacy of Eisenhower's government. Dulles went to Geneva unencumbered by any illusions about the political price to be paid for even a brief conference with Chou En-lai.

During the Geneva meeting Western diplomats were preoccupied with divisions among French, British, and American approaches to the Indochina fighting. The United States had previously sought British commitments to join an interventionist scheme if the French position crumbled further. Foreign Minister Eden objected to this idea, however, and maintained that to widen the war would be folly. France's difficult position, exemplified by the debacle at Dien Bien Phu, discrediting the Navarre plan, led London to assume that the war in the north was already lost; besides, the Commonwealth would oppose a seemingly procolonial British policy. The French government wanted to extricate itself rapidly and gracefully from defeat and, if possible, salvage some of its Southeast Asian possessions. As it was, Joseph Laniel's government toppled before popular dissatisfaction with the slowness and inconclu-

6. *Congressional Record*, January 14, 1954, pp. 232–33.

siveness of negotiations; Pierre Mendes-France's premiership barely escaped the same fate before accomplishing what Dulles termed its "disguised surrender." France gave up, not so much for military reasons as because two of its governments could not meet the cost and lacked internal support.

Despite preoccupations with Western difficulties, tensions among the communist delegations were apparent to British and American observers. The most obvious intracommunist problem was the divergence between the Viet Minh's ambitious aspirations—a united Vietnam under Ho's party—and those of Russia and China. By themselves, the Viet Minh probably could not conquer the entire country; and yet, unfortunately for Ho, the communist camp was not forthcoming with needed diplomatic aid. The Americans largely attributed Chinese caution to fears instilled by Dulles, who had repeatedly warned that Peking's intervention in the war would invite American retaliation anywhere and at any time of Washington's choosing. In view of the efforts being devoted to China's first five-year plan aimed at economic reconstruction, Mao was surely unwilling to risk another expensive and bloody war. American intelligence also recognized that to Peking, a united Vietnam under Viet Minh auspices might eventually threaten China's paramountcy in Southeast Asia.[7] And Washington understood that Kremlin interests in Indochina were not important enough to require pressing France severely. Why, after all, should the Soviets antagonize Paris, thus encouraging French interest in the European Defense Community?

Although their goals were understood to be essentially compatible, some tactical divergence between the mainland powers was perceived by Western analysts. To Dulles, the Soviets seemed to have assumed a stand more moderate than China's, and at one point he thought this might lead to a serious rift over support of the Viet Minh. He certainly suspected that seemingly minor disagreements between Chou and Molotov concealed deeper cleavages within the communist alliance. Dulles believed in particular that the Soviets wanted to avoid war at all costs and would resist Chinese moves that might lead in that direction; assuming that such a war could be averted, the Soviets would probably be content to let the Chinese seize the Indochinese states "one by one."[8]

French Prime Minister Laniel and Foreign Minister Georges Bidault felt certain that Moscow was becoming increasingly anxious about potential in-

7. Melvin Gurtov, "China's Perceptions of the Indochina Crisis, 1953-1954," in Gurtov (ed.), *Peking's Approach to Negotiation* (Washington, 1969), 21-25.
8. *FRUS, 1952-1954*, XIII (Pt. 1), 1334.

dependent Chinese activity in Southeast Asia: the Soviets "were deeply afraid that their Chinese friends might drag them into an adventure which they themselves did not at all desire."[9] Moreover, the French government believed that neither the Soviets nor the communist Vietnamese would welcome an extension of Chinese influence anywhere in Southeast Asia.

Molotov attempted to impress upon Foreign Minister Anthony Eden that both of them had an important role to play at the conference: that of intermediary between two hostile groups. Of the well-publicized Anglo-American differences, Eden later recalled remarks by Molotov to the effect that he had read in the local newspapers of serious disputes between Britain and the United States but that he disbelieved such stories: "I said he was right not to [believe the news accounts], because allies often have to argue their respective points of view. Molotov said, 'That is right, we have to do that amongst ourselves, too.' And he emphasized to me once again that China was very much her own master in these matters." Peking was, in fact, so much its own master that, in the view of the American Broadcasting Information Service, Moscow was eager to avoid responsibility for any Chinese actions in the Far East that might yield American wrath.[10]

Dulles especially was encouraged by intelligence gathered during the meetings from sources in Peking. Apparently, when American intrusion in Indochina seemed likely, Chou sought assurances from Molotov that the Soviet Union would intervene if America launched a war against China. The Soviet answer was ambiguous and noncommittal. Molotov replied that the Geneva negotiations "should be conducted in a way that military intervention, if it should take place, would not expand into a war on the mainland of China." Dissatisfied, Chou pushed for a definite reply and stressed to Molotov that the war clique in the United States might take steps impervious to Soviet or Chinese influence. After receiving new instructions from Moscow, Molotov stated that only if the United States attacked China with atomic weapons would Russia retaliate against America; in the event of a conventional Sino-American war, the Soviet Union would provide weapons, industrial products, and technical skills, but no men. The Soviets argued, "It is to the advantage of China that Soviet Russia should temporarily stand aside. She may force a quick end of the war by threatening to participate, may rally the

9. *Ibid.*, XVI, 435, 483, 520.
10. Anthony Eden, *Full Circle* (London, 1960), 121; *FRUS, 1952–1954*, XVI, 875; Robert Sutter, *China Watch: Toward Sino-American Reconciliation* (Baltimore, 1978), 34, 126.

support of Asiatic countries for China against aggression and may mobilize world opinion in favor of China." [11]

Clearly, the Russians hoped to maintain their alliance with China at minimal costs. Dulles believed that China's reaction was one of resentment: "They think the Russian comrades are somewhat selfish. If the United States does not make use of the atomic or hydrogen bomb, Soviet Russia will not be in danger and wants to stand aloof." Dulles felt heartened, and his hope that the communist alliance could be divided through pressure was reinforced. Yet, throughout the conference, he insisted that the American delegation not make public allegations of independent Chinese policy or Peking's displeasure with modest Soviet support. To do so, he feared, would encourage Asian wishful thinking that China was more Asian than communist and that reasonable accommodation could be reached with Peking. [12]

The intelligence community seemed to share many of the conclusions reached by Dulles at Geneva. A national intelligence estimate issued in mid-June predicted that in the event the United States destroyed most of China's military installations and capabilities, the Soviet Union would deploy bluffs and high rhetoric and would probably supply equipment to China, but that the USSR would refrain from joining in war against the United States and would urge China to meet whatever demands were imposed by American leaders. [13]

Despite China's problems with Russia, Geneva was an unqualified diplomatic success for Peking. The end of hostilities precluded any possibility that American bases would be established adjacent to, and hostile troops stationed along, China's southeastern border. Provision was made that an ideologically acceptable regime occupy the zone between the People's Republic and the Franco-American-backed government in Saigon. In addition, Chinese participation in the conference dignified Peking's claims to international prestige; settlement of Asian issues would henceforth require Chinese inclusion. Peking's self-esteem and satisfaction in having been treated as a great power were apparent in the *People's Daily* editorial of July 22: "For the first time as one of the Big Powers, the People's Republic of China joined the other major powers in negotiating on vital international problems and made a contribution of its own that won acclaim of wide sections of public opinion. The international status of the People's Republic of China as one of the big world

11. Dulles to Senator Knowland, June 30, 1954, Dulles Papers.
12. *Ibid.*; "Communist China—Policy and Problems," December 13, 1954, #793.00/12-1354, RG 59, NA; *FRUS, 1952–1954*, XVI, 621.
13. *Ibid.*, XIII (Pt. 2), 1709.

powers has gained universal recognition.'' Peking thereafter never lost an opportunity to portray itself as *the* Asian power championing all Asia against
the West. During one of the conference's recesses, Chou exploited recently
won goodwill by traveling to India for meetings with Nehru. Together on June
28, 1954, they proclaimed for the first time the five principles of coexistence,
adopted a year later by Asian and African leaders at Bandung. At the same
time, however, China's relationship with Moscow seemed to grow steadily
more ambiguous; if nothing else, the Soviets seemed to have been displeased
by the unexpected, considerable prestige that accrued to China as a result of
Chou's skillful performance at Geneva.

In early June, 1954, American intelligence reported that Chinese domestic
programs aimed at expanding and modernizing the military continued to benefit directly from Soviet assistance. Peking's dependence on Moscow was
predicted to last for a fair period, and maintenance of the alliance would probably continue as ''a dominant aspect of China's foreign policy.'' Taking
nothing for granted, though, Soviet leaders allegedly treated their Chinese ally
with extreme deference and refrained from issuing straight orders. Nevertheless, the intelligence analysts pointed out, Moscow's predatory policies in
northeastern Asia continued unabated to compromise Chinese sovereignty.
Meanwhile, the Americans had good reason to suspect that popular Chinese
resentment against Russia was mounting. According to Humphrey Trevel-
yan, Britain's ambassador to China, most Chinese disliked the Russians and
grumbled about unfair rates for goods exchanged. He told C. L. Sulzberger
of the New York *Times* that ordinary people in Peking were friendlier to the
ambassador on learning that he was British, not Russian.[14] Still, to the Chinese
government, the important question was whether the Soviets would support
Peking in completing the social revolution and eliminating Mao's foe on Taiwan. Again, as with the Soviet performance at Geneva and in Korea, the
Chinese were in for some sharp disappointments.

To the American government, neither the Korean truce nor the Geneva
Conference represented victories for the West. In fact, the Geneva Accords
''completed a major forward stride of communism which may lead to the loss
of Southeast Asia.'' Consequently, over the advice of the National Intelligence Board, Eisenhower's government undertook measures to bolster the
sagging Saigon regime. Aid to Bao Dai was increased, and clandestine op-

14. National Intelligence Estimate, ''Communist China's Power Potential Through 1957,''
June 3, 1954, *Declassified Documents Quarterly*, III (January–March, 1977), 5; Sulzberger, *Long
Row of Candles*, 1004.

erations in the North to disrupt and embarrass the communist regime were undertaken. By these policies the United States began to relieve France of its colonial obligations and hoped to smooth the way for French integration into the European Defense Community. (Ironically, in August of 1954 France refused to accept membership in the organization.) Meanwhile, because of the disquieting Geneva decisions, the Manila Treaty negotiations were hurried along. On September 8, 1954, a treaty was signed pledging the United States, Australia, New Zealand, Thailand, the Philippines, France, and Great Britain to Southeast Asian collective security. The Southeast Asia Treaty Organization (SEATO), destined for little accomplishment, was born.

Attempts to buttress a European ally's international prestige thus eventually led Washington to place itself in opposition to Ho's national, Marxist-inspired Vietnamese revolutionary movement. As mentioned, American efforts during the ensuing years to develop an effective, noncommunist popular alternative to Ho failed. And for at least a decade and a half after Geneva, the United States remained committed to checking a presumed southward Chinese thrust. Did Dulles, unlike the British, reject any idea that Ho's interests were distinct from China's and that he might emerge as an Asian version of Tito? Conclusive evidence, one way or the other, is not yet available. If Dulles did not distinguish greatly between Chinese and North Vietnamese interests, the obvious question is why, given the administration's perception of differences between Russia and China, there was not a similar understanding of separate national concerns among communist parties in Asia. Perhaps official Washington's understanding of the foreign national interest had been reduced, at least in Southeast Asia, to simple anticommunism. Probably a paucity of knowledge about traditional Chinese-Vietnamese antagonism also handicapped Dulles' understanding.

FIRST OFFSHORE ISLANDS CRISIS

For a brief period after the Korean armistice was signed and after Geneva, the Cold War in the Far East seemed to take a peaceful turn. Violence flared anew in early autumn 1954, however, when Chinese communist gunners commenced bombardment of nearby Nationalist-held offshore islands. Reunification of Chinese territory undoubtedly was an important motive behind communist attempts to assert sovereignty over Quemoy, the Tachen Islands, and Matsu. The threatening quality of American policy, as perceived in Peking, was also responsible for precipitating the crisis of 1954–1955. From

Peking's perspective, external security would be enhanced if the American-backed Nationalist forces were dislodged from their nearby offshore fortifications. In addition, the artillery attacks demonstrated Chinese resolve not to be intimidated by increased American support of Taiwan. Peking had probably been alarmed in July, 1954, when Washington revealed that plans to enter into a security pact with Taipei had been under study for some time and intimated that a mutual security treaty would shortly be signed. Chinese concern was certainly heightened in early September with the establishment of SEATO; the new pact must have seemed in Peking to strengthen the American-inspired ring of hostile states.

Actual capture of the offshore islands would end the Nationalist blockade, which was disruptive of Chinese shipping from Shanghai to Canton. The Nationalist guerrilla nuisance, operating from the islands, would also be eliminated. The New China News Agency explained: "Directed and protected by the aggressive junta in the U.S., the gang of Chiang traitors has been using these islands as an important base for plundering and seizing fishing boats and merchant ships on the seas, harassing the coastal areas of the mainland and menacing and undermining maritime shipping and the security of the people living along the coast."[15] Peking's control of the islands would also deprive the Nationalists of a staging area from which to launch their liberation campaign, which was imminent, according to the recently "unleashed" Chiang.

Unaided, the People's Republic could not vanquish the apparent threat emanating from Quemoy and Matsu; only with Soviet aid could China have forced an "imperialist" withdrawal to Taiwan. Yet to Peking's disappointment, Moscow withheld support at the critical moment. Preoccupied with West German entry into NATO, Soviet leaders feared Sino-American conflict in the Pacific would distract from crucial European matters and posed a danger threatening to mix Russia with China in a hopeless war against the United States. Soviet support was limited to periodic verbal harangues against Washington.

Throughout the crisis, China's leaders bravely maintained that they enjoyed unequivocal Soviet support. Inevitably, the fiction collapsed. In February, 1955, as part of a program to develop nuclear warheads suitable for guided missiles, the United States initiated a series of H-bomb tests; these tests were also useful reminders to the Chinese of the odds against them. Peking responded by declaring that Moscow's support was substantial enough to check

15. J. H. Kalicki, *The Pattern of Sino-American Crises* (London, 1975), 137.

any American aggression, no matter how gruesome the struggle. Mao emphatically exclaimed, "We can all perceive the great cooperation between China and the Soviet Union. There are no aggressive plans of imperialism which cannot be smashed. Should the imperialists start a war of aggression we, together with the whole world, would certainly wipe them off the surface of the globe." [16] But a Soviet spokesman only blandly affirmed the great friendship between the Chinese People's Republic and the Soviet Union. Soon thereafter, American pressures combined with Soviet warnings to Peking evidently helped make China heed the risks, and in May Chinese air and artillery bombardments of the islands ceased. Significantly, during this episode the Soviets had not exploited American problems in Asia by taking aggressive moves in Europe. According to the administration, limited Soviet-American understanding was more important to Kremlin leaders than close cooperation with Peking.

At the peak of the offshore islands crisis, Khrushchev, N. A. Bulganin, and other members of the Soviet collective leadership met with Chinese leaders in Peking, an unthinkable gesture during Stalin's time. There the Soviets not only finally relinquished control of Port Arthur but also dissolved the joint Sino-Soviet companies and pledged assistance to Peking's first five-year plan. Soviet aid to the new industrial and agricultural drives included a $130 million credit, technical advice, and help on a nonmilitary nuclear program. In exchange, the Soviets hoped to exact promises from the Chinese that they would exercise restraint in their dispute with Taipei and Washington over the offshore islands. To the Soviets, then, aid was essentially an inducement aimed at retaining Chinese obedience to Moscow.

The Mao-Khrushchev talks apparently caused considerable discomfort for the Soviet leadership. Khrushchev himself found direct dealing with his Chinese counterpart an ordeal, and in his memoirs he reveals a racialist predisposition, reflected and reinforced by his encounters with Mao. The tough Soviet party boss was partially overcome by an "atmosphere that was typically Oriental. Everyone was unbelievably courteous and ingratiating, but I saw through their hypocrisy . . . it was all too sickeningly sweet. The atmosphere was nauseating." With respect to Mao, Khrushchev brooded: "I was never sure that I understood what he meant. I thought at the time that it must have been because of some special traits in the Chinese character and the Chinese way of thinking." [17]

16. New York *Times*, February 23, 1955.
17. Khrushchev, *Khrushchev Remembers*, 466.

The Chinese too had reason to be less than delighted by their ally. According to statements made by Mao in 1964, the Russians again refused to discuss Mongolia. Moreover, Chinese requests for aid may have exceeded Soviet capacity and generosity. Khrushchev relates in his memoirs that during the 1954 meetings, "when our country was still hungry and poverty-ridden from the war, Chou En-lai asked, 'Perhaps you could make us a gift of a university?' " Khrushchev replied that the Soviet Union was also poor: "We may be richer than you, but the war has just ended and we are still not back on our feet."[18]

Furthermore, at a time when Moscow was seeking to reduce international problems and yet China was skirmishing with American-backed Nationalists off the coast, Mao and Khrushchev disagreed violently on the nature and probable outcome of war with the West. Khrushchev preached the virtues of restraint and caution and admonished the Chinese of the twin dangers of ridiculing the United States and disparaging it as a paper tiger. Once home, Khrushchev, again according to his memoirs, declared that Soviet conflict with China was inevitable.

The American intelligence community was enormously impressed by numerous "incredible reports" about a shocked Khrushchev and Bulganin, positively dazed by Chinese independence, intransigence, and uncontrollability. Chinese demands for Soviet assistance against the United States, it was also thought, went far beyond anything the sober Russians would ever chance. From Moscow, Ambassador Bohlen reported that despite their pledges to Chinese security, the Soviets were most unlikely to run serious risks to themselves for the sake of Chinese claims against Taiwan. And the NSC predicted that if the Chinese failed to be satisfied with Soviet aid or if the Soviets should be disappointed by Chinese misconduct, then Sino-Soviet relations would become precipitantly a good deal rougher. Subsequent security arrangements and Russian-Chinese military coordination were, in any case, unimpressive. One expert reports that joint military planning and maneuvers were never conducted.[19]

Dulles and Eisenhower recognized from the outset of the offshore islands crisis that Quemoy and Matsu were irrelevant to the security of either Taiwan

18. *Ibid.*, 465–66.
19. Robert Amory, Address; "The Current World Situation," March 29, 1955, *Declassified Documents Quarterly*, V (January–March, 1979), 25; Bohlen to secretary of state, October 2, 4, 1954, #793.00/10–254 and #793.00/10–454, RG 59, NA; NSC 5429/5, December 22, 1954, NSC File, Modern Military Branch, NA; Raymond Garthoff, *Sino-Soviet Military Relations* (New York, 1966), 88.

or the United States. Yet both political and diplomatic reasons persuaded the administration to support Chiang's efforts to retain the islands. In the fall of 1954, ceding more territory, no matter how insignificant, would be popularly regarded as still another victory for Moscow and Peking. To many critics, the administration had already acquiesced in the surrender of twelve million Vietnamese to communism. The China lobby was especially adamant in warning against renewed "appeasement" of totalitarianism in Asia. Henry Luce wrote to Eisenhower that "any slightest weakening in the position and posture of the United States as the forceful ally of all anti-Communists in Asia would . . . lead to disastrous consequences."[20] To Chiang, the islands were vital to future plans; their loss would constitute a major reverse of his operations waged against the mainland. He believed also that forfeiture of the islands would deal a severe psychological blow, albeit not directly endangering Taiwan, to the morale of his armed forces as damaging as a battlefield rout.

As we have seen, Anglo-American disagreement over Western policy toward China had been simmering long before the communist bombardment of the Matsu and Quemoy islands sparked a minor crisis in the Atlantic alliance. By promoting regular diplomatic and trade relations with Peking, London still hoped to safeguard Hong Kong and woo China away from Soviet influence, a policy viewed by Dulles in late 1954 with pure dismay. In any case, during the crisis, Soviet restraint of China was paralleled by Britain's counsel to the Americans against actions that might instigate World War III. Macmillan wrote in his diary, "Indeed, both Moscow and London are working (somewhat paradoxically) on the same lines and are trying to restrain their friends."[21] Above all else, though, Eisenhower's natural caution ultimately prevailed over the recommendations of senior political and military advisers, notably Walter Robertson and Admiral Arthur Radford, urging him to embark on what Eisenhower called "channels leading to war."

Authorizing the president to employ armed force in the defense of Taiwan, the Pescadores, and those island fortifications necessary for Taipei's defense, the Formosa Resolution was ambiguous regarding American commitments to Quemoy and Matsu. Would the Americans really act to save the inconsequential islands and risk full-scale war? The uncertainty enabled Washington to retain maximum flexibility toward a vulnerable Western salient. If necessary, the islands could be abandoned without loss of prestige by claiming that they were incidental to Taiwan's defense; yet a warning had been issued that

20. Luce to Eisenhower, January 22, 1955, Eisenhower Papers.
21. Macmillan, *Tides of Fortune*, 533.

military action would follow Chinese "recklessness." The resolution also placated Senator Knowland and Admiral Radford, who sought "decisive action" in support of the Chinese Republic. Finally, Syngman Rhee of Korea and Chiang—unable to conduct their "holy war" of liberation against the mainland as they insisted they would, given American blessings and support—were reasonably satisfied by American commitments embodied in the resolution and in subsequent actions. Chiang and his congressional supporters were thoroughly gratified by the president's remarks at a news conference in March that the United States would employ atomic weapons against strictly military targets on the mainland if Taiwan should be attacked. To his confidants, Eisenhower privately advised that there was no reason to fear China, at least for a decade; the country was poor and militarily weak and heavily dependent on a questionable ally.[22]

In December, the United States and Taiwan signed a defense treaty pledging the parties to mutual aid in resisting "armed attack and communist subversive activities directed from without against their territorial integrity and political stability." Because Chiang's regime was unacceptable to most Asian governments—the price of recognizing it against Peking's wishes was steep—the United States could not assure Taiwan's protection through a multilateral security pact and consequently had to enter into a bilateral treaty. Actual agreement was formalized only after Chiang promised Dulles that Taiwan recognized the defensive element of the pact and that the United States was not obliged to aid him if he undertook offensive military actions against the mainland.[23]

In the meantime, equivocal Soviet support of China, abundantly evident to American policy planners, indicated to them the validity of keeping up pressure along the Sino-Soviet periphery. Soviet caution may also have suggested to the United States that additional advantages could be gained by improving relations with Moscow. American intelligence reported during the first period of the offshore islands episode that communist policy in Asia was developed through joint Sino-Soviet consultation, "not by the dictation of Moscow." Despite Soviet preponderance, Chinese influence within the alliance was understood to be rising inexorably. Friction between the allies would steadily increase as China exerted greater independent authority. Nevertheless, lead-

22. Memorandum, "Discussion at the 271st Meeting of the NSC," December 23, 1955, Eisenhower Papers.
23. Memorandum of conversation, October 18, 1954, RG 59, NA.

ership rivalry was not expected to debilitate the alliance, at least not in the immediate foreseeable future.

U.S. intelligence thought the Soviets were pursuing dual long-range goals. Theoretically at least, Moscow desired a Chinese ally that was both strong and reliable. Yet Russia, exercising communist command in Asia, evidently hoped to keep China both economically and militarily dependent; the October accords were read in Washington as indicating Khrushchev's keenness for retaining Chinese compliance. Peking's aggressive proclivities especially disturbed the Soviets, who appreciated that "communist China possesses capability for some independent action, even action which the U.S.S.R. might disapprove but which it would find difficult to repudiate." [24] The nature and timing of attacks against Nationalist territory were precisely a case in point.

In March, 1955, as the United States tested more H-bombs, American intelligence submitted the following assessment: in case of Sino-American clashes, both Peking and Moscow would try to contain the spread of hostilities, and the Soviet Union, although providing China with political and military support, would avoid direct military involvement. Intelligence analysts were divided, however, over the likely Soviet response should Moscow come to believe that American actions threatened Peking's survival. Possibly the Soviets would intervene while acting to limit hostilities to the Far East. Or perhaps Soviet armies would remain aloof, as they had during the Korean War. In either case, the joint intelligence staff agreed that Soviet leaders, aware of their country's small nuclear stockpiles and inadequate delivery capabilities, would not hazard Russia's survival for China in war against the United States. [25] The analysts appreciated, moreover, that if Russia was unwilling to chance, at least bluff, Moscow for Peking, the alliance's value to China was dubious indeed.

The NSC concluded in March that within the next five years neither the Soviet Union nor China would deliberately initiate or risk a war that might involve the United States; even Chinese military probing of Taiwan and attacks against the offshore islands would be limited, lest the Americans were antagonized into full-scale war. And yet the NSC believed that the mainland states would use every means short of war to dislodge American influence

24. National Intelligence Estimate: "Communist Courses of Action in Asia Through 1957," November 23, 1954, Declassified Documents Quarterly, III (January–March, 1977), 3.

25. National Intelligence Estimate: "Communist Capabilities and Intentions with Respect to the Offshore Islands and Taiwan, 1955," March 16, 1955, Declassified Documents Quarterly, I (January–March, 1975), 1.

from Asia and weaken Washington's allies by a blend of subversion and military pressure.

The NSC was equally confident that the Sino-Soviet bloc would confront problems aplenty, both strategic and political. For example, the Soviets had to police Eastern Europe, itself chafing as agricultural and consumer production lagged. Further, despite bonds of ideology with China and shared fears over the United States, the Kremlin was anxious about retaining Mao within the Soviet-led bloc. The NSC therefore resolved that Washington should be prepared, as ever, to exploit differences between the communist states.[26] Limited *ad hoc* negotiations with Chinese leaders might even serve American purposes in weakening Sino-Soviet ties; we shall see later, though, that such innovations in policy did not advance far.

In the meantime, Dulles told the Advertising Club of New York that Chinese actions were more provocative of war than the Soviet Union's. The secretary also explained to newsmen in March—no doubt with his Kremlin audience in mind—that Soviet support for China in its confrontation with America was an expensive proposition and carried the risk of general war. He also emphasized the monumental expense to the Soviet Union of supplying weapons to China. Dulles thus played on Soviet fears of a Chinese bogey, expensive to maintain as an ally and dangerous if it should drag Russia into an unwanted war against the United States. Dulles accurately predicted to the president in May that "the Soviets may put increasing pressure upon the Chinese Communists to avoid war."[27]

GENEVA, 1955

According to Prime Minister Eden, "The Geneva meeting was worthwhile if only for the discreet improvement it brought about in the Formosa Strait. By the end of the conference, the Foreign Secretary and I were convinced that all present would have been sincerely happy to see the offshore islands sunk under the sea." Except for this slight advance, the July conference produced little tangible resolution of outstanding East-West problems. Behind solemn declarations about the desirability of peace in the nuclear age and the touting of a new Geneva spirit stood the stubborn fact that Europe was divided into two opposing military pacts. The discussion of various issues—the Soviet disarmament plan, Eisenhower's "open skies" scheme, German reunifica-

26. NSC 5440/1, December 28, 1954, NSC File, Modern Military Branch, NA.
27. Dwight D. Eisenhower, *Mandate for Change* (London, 1963), 478–79.

tion, and the Soviet occupation of Eastern Europe—was predictably inconclusive. Dulles, in rare understatement, told the press, "There are probably long arduous months ahead in which we must expect disappointments" before the "ultimate achievement of a secure peace." Still, the conference was significant, for its convocation symbolized Soviet and American recognition of the dangers inherent in prolonged antagonism. If nothing else, the Geneva exercise in international amity caused a temporary deescalation in the violent Soviet-American war of words.[28]

The peaceful sentiments expressed by Soviet and American leaders at Geneva were realized in subsequent limited political cooperation such as the establishment of cultural exchange programs. Superpower restraint was also advanced at the summit meeting. In 1956, when Soviet and Warsaw Pact forces "saved" Hungary from "capitalist counterrevolution," the United States responded simply by voicing disapproval in the United Nations and was prepared to do little else for Poland. Similarly, the Soviet reaction to the tripartite attack on Egypt by French, British, and Israeli forces was marked only by self-righteous denunciations. Although Khrushchev's language was particularly vitriolic and by innuendo he made a nuclear threat, it was American pressure, not Soviet, that forced the allies to end their offensive. And in 1958, Moscow's commitment to improved relations with the West again resulted in Soviet pressures on China to defuse the second offshore islands crisis.

Even before the July Geneva meetings, the Americans seriously doubted Peking's appreciation of Moscow as a trustworthy representative of Chinese interests. Dulles believed, moreover, that the Russian leaders would have to push Chinese demands (U.S. troop withdrawal from Korea, retirement of Seventh Fleet ships from the Taiwan Straits, and UN membership), thereby demonstrating once and for all that the Soviet Union was a loyal, useful ally.[29]

The British government, too, was alert. At the conference, Macmillan discerned extreme Soviet nervousness about the People's Republic. He recorded on July 15 that the collective leadership was anxious about China and made no effort to hide the fact from him: "They (like us) wish that Quemoy and Matsu could sink beneath the sea. They may fear—in the long run—that China will be a danger to their eastern flank." He also felt that the Soviets would have preferred "a weak nationalist or capitalist China which they could plunder to a Communist China which they have to assist." After an Anglo-Soviet

28. Eden, *Full Circle*, 311; New York *Times*, July 26, 1955; Louis Halle, *The Cold War as History* (London, 1971), 334.
29. "Soviet Goals at Geneva," April, 1955, Dulles Papers.

dinner meeting, Macmillan recorded that the Russians were not at all "keen" on China, regarded it as a drain on both their industrial and military resources, and wondered when China would pose a threat to Russian security in Siberia. Later, during his post-Geneva visit with Khrushchev in Moscow, Chancellor Konrad Adenauer of Germany was quizzed by a plaintive-sounding chairman on how best to handle the Chinese problem. The Soviet leader complained, "China already has 600 million inhabitants, who live on a handful of rice. Each year there are 12 million more. How is that going to end? I beg you to help us to resolve our difficulties with China."[30]

Dulles believed that, as indicated at Geneva, "the Soviet leaders did not want reversion to sharp Russian-American antagonism and . . . they will pay some appreciable price to avoid it."[31] If necessary, China might even be expendable.

Shortly after the Geneva Conference, Nelson Rockefeller, special assistant to the president, coordinated a study titled *Psychological Aspects of U.S. Strategy*. Rockefeller and his committee determined that the Chinese communists were especially vulnerable on the basis of their militant nationalism. Contrasting Sino-American enmity with decreased Soviet-American hostility, they also stressed the importance of achieving a *modus vivendi* with Russia. After all, the Soviet Union, not China, posed a strategic threat. Soviet actions and press statements also revealed Moscow's fear of nuclear war and her willingness to reject Chinese-inspired adventures.[32]

Beginning in July, American propaganda started to exploit Soviet fears observed by Western leaders at Geneva. One VOA commentator explained, "The cause of their [Sino-Soviet] conflict of interest lies in one great fact—the fact that China suffers from chronic and increasing overpopulation, while the Soviet Union, relatively speaking, is under-populated. What makes this contrast more striking is the fact that the most underpopulated areas of the Soviet Union are those closest to China." Another American broadcast cited Adenauer's remarks in August in the Swiss newspaper *Der Bund* to the effect that China had a yearly birth rate of millions: "In the near future the [Chinese] People's Republic will no longer have enough territory. It cannot expand to the South. It must move North in order to continue to live, and that means into the Russian Asiatic territories." The commentator finished by prophesying almost

30. Macmillan, *Tides of Fortune*, 619; Andre Fontaine, *History of the Cold War*, I (2 vols., London, 1965), 133.

31. "United States Post-Geneva Policy," August 15, 1955, Dulles Papers.

32. "Discrete Problems of the Far East," *Psychological Aspects of U.S. Strategy: Source Book* (N.p., 1955), 67.

cheerfully that a future "trouble spot" would develop along the Sino-Soviet border. Meanwhile, through varied other covert operations—their nature not now known—the United States continued efforts to impair relations between the USSR and Communist China.[33]

AMERICA'S REBUFF OF CHINESE OVERTURES

Twice, in 1954 and 1955, China emerged from isolation and joined in the Geneva Peace Conference and the Asian-African meeting at Bandung. During both conferences but especially at Bandung, Chinese prestige increased appreciatively. There, under Chou En-lai, Peking's delegation affirmed support for Asian and African peoples struggling against imperialism. Soviet principals Khrushchev and Bulganin, perturbed that Russia had not been asked to send a representative to the conference, soon afterward undertook a policy of cultivating relations with Egypt and India. Thus the specter of Chinese-Soviet competition in Asia and Africa was evident as early as 1955.

The Bandung declaration of *panch shila* (the five principles were mutual respect for territorial integrity and sovereignty, nonaggression, noninterference in each other's internal affairs, equality and mutual benefit, and peaceful coexistence) provided the background for the launching of a strenuous Chinese campaign to improve relations with the United States. As an immediate gesture of goodwill, Radio Peking announced that the families of American servicemen in Chinese jails could visit their loved ones and stay in facilities sponsored by the Red Cross. Then Chou, whose virtuoso performance at Bandung set the conference's pace and style, declared on April 23, 1955, that "the Chinese people are friendly to the American people." Besides desiring peace, "the Chinese government is willing to sit down and enter into negotiations with the U.S. government to discuss the question of relaxing tension in the Taiwan area."[34]

The State Department's initial conditions for Sino-American talks were plainly unacceptable to the People's Republic and indicated Washington's want of seriousness. The United States insisted that Taiwan should have equal representation with the United States and China at the proposed meetings; Peking was also expected to participate in UN Security Council meetings aimed at ending hostilities around Taiwan. The implied recognition of Taiwan as

33. Voice of America, "China's Population and Soviet Empty Space," July 18, 1955; *ibid.*, "Peiping's Interest in Outer Mongolia," August 25, 1955; NSC 5412/2, December 28, 1955, NSC File, Modern Military Branch, NA.
34. New York *Times*, April 24, 1955.

equal and legitimate was, of course, anathema to Peking. And the suggestion that Peking send representatives to an international body that had repeatedly denied her membership and condemned her as an aggressor and in which her arch-rival played a significant role could not be sincere. Indeed, Dulles was suspicious that the friendly Chinese stance was merely a pose chiefly for propaganda purposes. He feared that a conciliatory Chinese posture toward the United States was intended merely to demonstrate to Asian and African leaders the new moderate orientation of Peking's policy. An incensed Chou responded by scolding the State Department for cleaving to unsound policies and cautioned that China's willingness to negotiate with the United States did not deflect Peking from opposing imperialism or from plans to liberate Taiwan.

Sensing an opportunity, though, Dulles soon cautiously signaled that negotiations with Russia's increasingly burdensome ally might begin, and belligerent Chinese propaganda against the United States declined noticeably. At the same time, various governments having diplomatic relations with Peking indicated to Dulles their belief that China was anxious to improve matters with Washington. The NSC was also entirely open to the idea that acceptable, enforceable agreements with China—over limited issues certainly, perhaps even over general ones—were possible. Consequently, the secretary declared that the United States could not forever "take a purely negative position" toward China and that limited negotiations between the two countries might be to their mutual advantage, especially in regard to such issues as the "citizens of the two countries held by the other."[35]

Dulles then stated that if a Taiwan cease-fire should be initiated, perhaps wider Sino-American negotiations could follow. He also reported to some journalists that definite signs were appearing that suggested China was beginning to exercise initiative independent of the Soviet Union.[36] Yet for the sake of his domestic constituency, the secretary emphasized that in any forthcoming discussions Taiwan's fate would not be decided "behind its back." Shortly thereafter, Eisenhower expressed hopes that productive discussions aimed at increasing Far Eastern stability might emerge. And the intensity of the Straits crisis abruptly subsided, as both Peking and Washington took actions to improve the climate for negotiations. Dulles announced that a cease-fire would not be viewed as Peking's renunciation of claims to Taiwan; in turn,

35. "Estimate of Prospects of Soviet Union Achieving Its Goals," April, 1955, Dulles Papers.
36. "For the Press," No. 231, April 26, 1955, Dulles Papers.

Chou reiterated the desirability of acquiring Taiwan through nonmilitary means.

In late July, both governments announced the beginning of Sino-American ambassadorial-level talks in Geneva. So-called practical matters and the problem of American prisoners in China were scheduled for discussion. Peking next proclaimed its intention to release captured American airmen incarcerated since the Korean War. In September, Ambassador Wang, Chinese representative to Czechoslovakia, and U. Alexis Johnson, American ambassador to Poland, announced an agreement that permitted all Chinese citizens in America and all American citizens in China to repatriate if they so desired. At roughly the same time, in August, the administration examined the possibility of exporting foods and cotton to China.[37]

To the Chinese, discussion about the repatriation issue was merely a pretext for initiating talks of a more comprehensive nature. Ambassador Wang announced on the first day of the meetings that China hoped to elevate them to the foreign-minister level as soon as possible. A few days later, he explained that once the nationals' problem was settled, the talks should concentrate on major topics such as establishment of diplomatic relations, cultural and trade exchanges, Peking's membership in the United Nations, American withdrawal of military forces on Taiwan, and so forth. With the exception of the issue of prisoners, however, the American negotiators did not express interest in exploring problems of underlying significance.

From the administration's standpoint, the release of American prisoners of war added to its popular standing, but substantive agreements with China were politically unfeasible. Dulles and Eisenhower were not about to try further the patience and good humor of their supporters, particularly Senators Knowland and Welker. At one point the former had demanded that Chiang's government be represented at any conference attended by delegates from Peking and Washington and had declared, "The policy of this government is not to barter away the territory of any country without its presence at the negotiations." Congressman Judd wanted to know why "international gangsters" should be consulted about problems in maintaining global order, and McCarthy warned against a U.S. sellout of its Nationalist ally.[38]

Prime Minister Eden and his government were especially disappointed. And

37. "Potential Markets in the Sino-Soviet Bloc for U.S. Surplus Agricultural Products," August 12, 1955, Box 8, Francis Papers.

38. Foster Rhea Dulles, *American Policy Toward Communist China, 1949–1969* (New York, 1972), 141.

Adlai Stevenson blamed the China bloc for once again thwarting Sino-American negotiations; he labeled this the "greatest political crime of our times." Dulles had indeed responded hastily to critics accusing him of softness, appeasement, and retreat. In November, he submitted to the public that Peking's "use of U.S. hostages as pawns" demonstrated Chinese insincerity and treachery. The retention of nineteen remaining American prisoners apparently constituted an insuperable barrier between the two states.[39]

By the end of the year, the Chinese again raised tensions in the Taiwan Straits by increasing propaganda activities and resuming limited artillery action. According to State Department intelligence, Peking was trying, rather clumsily, to force the United States into accepting a Sino-American foreign ministers meeting.[40]

In January, 1956, the State Department suggested that the use of force in settling Sino-American disputes would not always remain a realistic option, but no mention was made of a future end to U.S. involvement with Taiwan or even of the possibility of reducing aid to Chiang. In a period of supposedly developing negotiations, few other American statements implying continued involvement in internal Chinese affairs could have more antagonized Peking. That same month, Dulles again reviewed his policy toward China for Britain's new foreign secretary, Selwyn Lloyd, and indicated that Western goals would suffer if London or Washington set out to win the goodwill of Chinese leaders or if British and American policies toward China continued to diverge.

Although discouraged, the Chinese determined to progress toward an understanding with Washington. Peking once again suggested that the ambassadorial-level talks should be elevated, to which Secretary Dulles vaguely replied that only a "meaningful renunciation of force" and release of all American prisoners could facilitate relations. As various analysts have argued, the return of prisoners could have been easily accomplished within the context of an overall agreement. But Chinese failure to return the prisoners was largely interpreted by the American public as reflecting Peking's bad faith. Even if the prisoners should be released, the administration could still claim that Peking had not made appropriate moves toward a true renunciation of force. As a result, the proposed foreign ministers' meetings, which if held would have constituted tacit recognition of the People's Republic, were un-

39. *Ibid.*
40. Office of Intelligence Research, Department of State; "Asian Communist Orbit," January, 1956, RG 59, NA.

dermined. The ambassadorial talks continued for years but without major significance.

Both American political parties in 1956 included in their campaign platforms resolutions declaring hostility to future Chinese bids for UN admission and affirmed the soundness of nonrecognition. Respecting China's admission to the United Nations, the Democrats, despite Stevenson's private wishes, declared, "We pledge determined opposition to the admission of the Communist Chinese into the United Nations [and] urge a continuing effort to effect the release of all Americans detained by Communist China." The Republicans took a similar tough stand and piously promised "to oppose the seating of Communist China in the UN, thus upholding international morality." In the meantime, aid to Taiwan continued at ever-increasing levels. Earlier auguries that a thaw in Sino-American relations might appear thus came to nothing. As Dulles reminded his audiences in 1956 in one of his favorite adages, "One swallow does not make a summer." Nonetheless, the secretary must have been privately confident that his apparent receptiveness to Chinese overtures, no matter how qualified or hesitant, had startled and worried Russian leaders.

The material now available clearly demonstrates two things about the events and American foreign policy for the years 1954 and 1955. First, the concept that the United States could and should work to undermine Sino-Soviet cooperation had great staying power and, despite various setbacks, persisted in the minds of top policy makers. An internal administration briefing paper, composed in December, 1954, reaffirmed that "it would be in the interests of the United States to bring about a split between Communist China and the USSR." Second, the Eisenhower administration was willing to consider more than one option. Arthur Dean, for example, strongly advocated improved relations with China as a means of weakening its exclusive reliance on Russia; Eisenhower and Dulles also seem to have at least flirted with such an idea. But to have pursued this course during the McCarthy period was very nearly impossible.

Dulles was satisfied to retain Taiwan as a client and apply military and political pressure on China. As stated in the December briefing paper, "The policy of keeping Communist China under the feasible maximum of pressures would appear to be the best means of generating an internal crisis (which would be favorable to a Sino-Soviet rupture) by the frustration of her economic aims and her expansionist aims." Although such a rupture was not immediately in the offing, "sources of friction and weakness in the alliance are thought to exist in the paucity of Soviet economic aid, in Moscow's apparent reluctance to go along with Communist China's plan for 'liberating' Formosa, and in the long-standing antipathy between the Chinese and Russian peoples."[41] Dulles hoped, and subsequent events were to prove him correct, that both Chinese aid requirements of Russia for domestic modernization and support in foreign affairs would burden the communist alliance beyond endurance.

41. "Communist China—Policy and Problems," December 13, 1954, #793.00/12-1354, RG 59, NA.

EPILOGUE

Evolving Sino-Soviet relations, marked by asymmetrical Russian and Chinese economic and military development, initially stabilized as a dependency relationship. Temporarily at least, Chinese security was guaranteed by Soviet commitments to Peking's industrial, technological, and military construction. But by 1955, the Soviet Union had demonstrated the limits of its support. Financial and technical aid was not especially generous, and Soviet reliability as an ally was problematic. Moscow had lent embarrassingly inadequate support in the revolution and in Korea. Also, the contrast between Chinese wisdom and military prowess and Soviet mismanagement and caution during the Korean War probably suggested to Mao his own superiority over the post-Bolshevik Russian regime. But the postwar world, characterized by extreme bipolarization, dictated that undeveloped China side with the one country capable of deterring renewed acts of "imperial aggression."

It is clear that the initial American response to the Sino-Soviet alliance conformed to classical diplomacy's *modus operandi*. The United States attempted to divide its enemy by drawing China, the weaker party, away from Russia. Yet for assorted domestic reasons, American policy could not be too openly considerate of the Chinese communists. Chinese suspicions of the United States, mutual misunderstanding, and the demands of allies (Taiwan in the case of America, Russia in that of China) also helped undermine Acheson's necessarily subtle policy. Beginning with Sino-American fighting in Korea, the United States on the whole was rougher on China, regarding it as militant, inadmissible, and unrecognizable. At the same time, the United States expanded its negotiations agenda with Moscow. And while seeking a relaxation of Soviet-American tension, the United States sought to diminish presumed Soviet profit by squeezing the communist alliance very hard and thereby hastening the day of its demise. Though American policy was not ultimately responsible for the shattering of Sino-Soviet cooperation, by early 1956 the Dulles-Eisenhower version of containment, of applied pressure, seems to have contributed, as its authors hoped, to the weakening of Russian and Chinese pledges to each other.[1]

As was evident from the Twentieth Congress of the Soviet party in February, 1956, the prospect of massive American retaliation against the mainland communist states had helped erode Russian commitments to Chinese security. Identifying Soviet foreign policy with Marxist-Leninist strategic principles, Khrushchev formally adopted a policy—previously expressed by Stalin (1952) and Malenkov (1953)—"sensitive to the evolving international system." Lenin's doctrine on the inevitability of war between the socialist and capitalist camps was modified as not entirely relevant because of "epoch making changes" since World War II. Instead, socialism would defeat the decadent West through competitive coexistence, parliamentary methods, and the superior communist model exemplified by the Soviet Union.

The policy of peaceful coexistence was to serve immediate and long-term Soviet goals, foremost of which was avoiding nuclear war with the United States. To this end, Khrushchev conspicuously omitted making promises to support revolutionary struggles at the Twentieth Congress. Although later forced to revise his stand because of Chinese criticisms, Khrushchev remained fearful that too active support for liberation movements in anticolonial wars would lead to their escalation and direct Soviet confrontation with the United States. Perhaps, too, the theory of peaceful transition aided nonruling communist parties by soothing Western and Third World leaders' fears of internal subversion controlled by Moscow. In Europe a reduction of East-West tensions might also enable the Soviet Union to press its claims against Germany and a less vigilant West. Furthermore, as previously mentioned, reduced Soviet-American tensions would permit the Soviet Union to curtail expensive arms development, thereby making limited resources available to long-neglected domestic programs. Thus, that war was not inevitable and should be avoided for communism's sake and that socialism could be advanced through nonviolent means were ideologically phrased principles supporting

1. NSC 5602, February 8, 1956, NSC File, Modern Military Branch, NA.

Soviet goals of self-interest: avoiding war and expanding communism at risks minimal to the Soviet Union.

China viewed the Soviet policy of peaceful coexistence as a setback for communism and, more important, an indirect threat to Chinese security. American hostility to the People's Republic, demonstrated by aggression in Korea, interference in the uncompleted revolution, and continued rebuffs to Peking's overtures for improved relations and a UN seat, was not lost on the Chinese leadership. Consequently, Soviet policy modifications inspired Chinese apprehensions that in any future Sino-American crisis Soviet reactions would be circumspect and limited to minimal support.[2] Perhaps the Soviet Union would even sacrifice its fraternal ally to American imperialism to assure Soviet safety. The Chinese responded by warning that world peace was still threatened by Western imperialism and that socialist security depended on unity and continued vigilance.

Khrushchev's policy of peaceful coexistence, then, initiated the ideologically expressed Sino-Soviet disagreement, rooted in separately perceived national security interests. Despite Mao's claimed adherence to the principle of Soviet leadership of the socialist camp, China's forceful polemic eventually threatened to diminish Soviet leadership, based as it was on presumed philosophical insight and experience-informed wisdom.

Non-American-related, intracommunist problems also strained relations between Peking and Moscow in the mid-1950s. Eli Ginzberg, director of the Conservation of Human Resources at Columbia University, reported directly to Eisenhower the observations of an Israeli delegation that toured China extensively in 1955. Ginzberg stressed, "There is considerable evidence of friction between the Chinese and the Russians." Informed Chinese citizens apparently felt bitterly that the terms of Russia's trade with the People's Republic on the one hand and with the European communist bloc on the other were unfairly rigged against China. Ginzberg also reported that the Israelis were impressed by seeing that nationals from Eastern Europe were monitored and restricted by Chinese officials in a manner that was no more gracious than that inflicted upon other Europeans, such as the British or French. Not only were Russians subject to local police surveillance, but they were also the object of popular resentment: "In the South the feeling of hostility toward the Russians is sufficiently great so that the members of the Israeli Mission were given police protection for fear that they might be roughly handled by a crowd

2. Hinton, *China's Turbulent Quest*, 79–80.

that mistook them for Russians.'' It was therefore understandable that Soviet advisers tried not to irritate Chinese sensibilities: ''In visits to factories where there were Russian experts, the Israelis reported that the Russians were always careful to point out in answer to questions that they were not in charge, and would refer to a local Chinese manager.''[3]

Observations made by the Israeli delegation were supplemented by Allen Whiting's findings published in the October, 1955, edition of *Far Eastern Survey*. Whiting, one of the best postwar American analysts of China, wrote, ''Despite confident claims from Peking and Moscow of the 'invincible, unshakable, and perpetual solidarity of Sino-Soviet friendship,' certain groups in Communist China remain dubious about complete and exclusive reliance upon the Soviet Union. Chinese Communist publications reveal recurring patterns of misgivings concerning the Russian 'elder brother' who is to teach 'New China' all things from art to zoology.'' The disgruntled groups included members of the intelligentsia and industrial cadres vexed by Soviet arrogance and conceit.

Khrushchev's policy of destalinization, also inaugurated at the Twentieth Congress, caused further problems between the CCP and CPSU. By the admission of its own leadership, the Fatherland of Socialism was fallible, and the former chief of all progressive peoples was guilty of perpetrating crimes and murder. The legitimacy of Soviet leadership in the communist world, based on the supposed rich experience and wisdom of the Soviet Union, was thus shaken. In Eastern Europe the power of the ''little Stalins'' was gravely weakened by Khrushchev's revelations and their authority undermined. The resulting dissension there produced confusion in Moscow and so lowered the prestige of the CPSU that, at least according to Peking, Chinese assistance in 1956 and 1957 was essential to maintaining Soviet power in Eastern Europe. The Chinese leadership later claimed credit for restraining Khrushchev from carrying out harsh military reprisals against Poland (on grounds that they were unnecessary), while boasting that it was Chinese insistence that finally forced a hesitant and frightened Soviet government to intervene in Hungary. Whether or not such claims are true, there is no doubt that Chou En-lai's visits to Moscow, Warsaw, and Budapest in 1957 helped calm an explosive situation and were aimed principally at rehabilitating Soviet prestige. Khrushchev clearly became indebted to Peking for its aid in Eastern Europe; despite Mao's un-

3. Eli Ginzberg to President Eisenhower, March 5, 1956, Official File 168, Eisenhower Library.

equivocal verbal support for the Warsaw Pact, Khrushchev may also have suspected that Chinese intentions included supplanting Soviet leadership.

In China, Khrushchev's attacks on Stalin's cult of personality suggested to Mao's local opponents a convenient and indirect method by which to reduce his immense, similarly elevated position. At the Eighth Congress of the CCP, references to "the thought of Mao Tse-tung" were struck from the constitution, and the title of general secretary was given to a rival of Mao's, Teng Hsia-p'ing. Mao meanwhile responded by trying to undermine the assumptions on which criticisms of his rule were based. To this end he initiated the "One Hundred Flowers" early in 1957, which eventually resulted in anti-Mao criticisms so severe that the embarrassed leadership abruptly ended the campaign in June. Soviet destalinization therefore adversely affected Mao's party position and led ultimately to humiliating countrywide censure of his authority. He could hardly be blamed for resenting Khrushchev, who had failed even to consult with him before embarking on a course that was bound to have far-reaching repercussions on Chinese communism and on the world movement.

Later, during the second Quemoy crisis in 1958, China appears to have deliberately maneuvered the Soviet Union dangerously close to confrontation with the United States, perhaps again testing Soviet commitments to China. Still, the Soviets resisted Chinese pressures and took virtually no public position until after the crisis had passed. In 1963, a Chinese spokesman derided the feebleness of Soviet support: "Although the situation in the Taiwan Straits was tense, there was no possibility that a nuclear war would break out and no need for the Soviet Union to support China with its nuclear weapons. It was only when they were clear that this was the situation that Soviet leaders expressed their support for China." Russian and American desires to resolve the German issue and reach an arms agreement remained intact during the crisis and demonstrated anew to China's leaders the waywardness of their fraternal ally. According to Edward Freers, former chief of the State Department's East European Desk, Dulles knew about Soviet and Chinese differences during the 1958 crisis and fashioned his strategy accordingly.[4] A combination of military threat and diplomatic pressure toward the communist states resulted in meager, marginal Soviet support of Peking.

During the last remaining years of the Eisenhower administration, the communist alliance crumbled quickly, and attempts to salvage it were submerged by a crush of international events and by Russia's ambivalent support

4. Gittings, *Survey of the Sino-Soviet Dispute*, 92; Edward Freers, Dulles Oral History, Mudd Library, Princeton University, Princeton, N.J.

of Chinese modernization. In response to China's "Great Leap Forward" and the coinciding campaign to develop modern military forces, the Soviets sent fourteen hundred technicians and advisers; according to Chinese accounts, Khrushchev also promised, but did not supply, Chinese scientists with a sample atomic bomb. Very likely, as at least one observer has stated, Soviet assistance during this period was an act of coalition diplomacy to ensure Chinese support of Soviet leadership and to encourage them in a moderate foreign policy. The abject failure of this tactic, of course, was illustrated by the second Quemoy crisis and vociferous Chinese polemics against the policy of peaceful coexistence.

In 1959, amid speculations about Soviet-American detente and the trumpeting of a new "Camp David spirit," the Chinese leadership became deeply suspicious of superpower cooperation and even of their possible collusion against the People's Republic. The proposed 1960 Paris summit meeting between Eisenhower and Khrushchev precipitated a violent Chinese response significantly elevating the intensity of the Peking-Moscow quarrel. Chinese spokesmen warned against the dangers of negotiating with the still-murderous imperialists and claimed that although a peaceful resolution of global contradictions was a possibility, socialist humanity would survive if war should occur and, with the debris of capitalism, could build an even greater, flourishing communist society.

The U-2 incident in 1960, after which the Soviets canceled the Paris conference, vindicated the Chinese in their long-held position on the treacherous nature of Western imperialism. Forsaking prudence, Chinese representatives openly criticized the Soviet party in various international communist meetings and did so even at the 1960 Moscow conference of ruling Marxist parties. In turn, the Chinese criticisms were vigorously contested by Soviet polemicists, who stressed Lenin's advocacy of peaceful coexistence to assure socialist survival and prosperity. Later that same year, Khrushchev's indignation with Chinese criticisms, which were becoming increasingly personal, and Peking's lack of cooperation led him to terminate all Soviet aid programs in China; he also withdrew all Soviet advisers, many of whom took with them blueprints of half-finished factories. Moscow probably hoped this unilateral action would force China to return to properly obedient and respectful behavior.

While the ideological debate escalated, events after the Eisenhower-Dulles era contributed to a marked increase in Sino-Soviet problems. The Chinese roundly condemned the Soviets for their 1962 debacle in Cuba; and when limited post-Cuban Soviet-American detente culminated in the Test Ban Treaty in 1963, Chinese and Soviet enmity burst into the open: the Chinese accused Khrushchev of unmitigated, unholy revisionism, while the Soviets lambasted Peking as hell-bent on precipitating nuclear war. Subsequent competitive Sino-Soviet aid to North Vietnam, the pronounced anti-Soviet aspect of the Cultural Revolution, and the Russian invasion of Czechoslovakia radically worsened matters between the former allies. By the early 1970s, relations had deteriorated to such a point (fighting had occurred along the border, and uncommon spontaneous demonstrations were held before the Chinese embassy in Moscow) that some informed analysts predicted a full-scale war would break out between China and the Soviet Union. In fact, the Soviet government approached the Nixon administration on its attitude should the Russians attack and destroy China's nuclear installations. A conflict thus developed between the largest communist states in which the magnitude of dispute was essentially greater than the sum of its parts. Foreign policy disagreements, mutual domestic interference, dissimilar domestic experiences, ideological conflict, and to some extent American actions in the 1950s had rent asunder a fragile partnership.

Although it is impossible to deny American policy makers of the 1949–1955 period some perspicacity and cleverness with regard to the Sino-Soviet alliance, despite formidable domestic constraints, it is essential to recognize the role of these leaders in creating the bugaboo of aggressive international communism that led to McCarthyism and greatly handicapped adroit diplomacy.

President Truman became convinced in the winter of 1946–1947 that a dispassionate analysis of Europe's vulnerability to the Soviet Union was inadequate for persuading Congress or the public to support an American policy reorientation as significant as that embodied by the Marshall Plan and Truman Doctrine. A January, 1947, poll indicated that 40 percent of the American public thought Russia could still be trusted. And almost 75 percent believed the United States was as much to blame for global problems as the Soviet Union. Unless something was done, popular support would lag behind planned policies aimed against the Soviets. In Clark Clifford's words, the administration had to "bring people up to [the] realization that the war isn't over by any means."[5] Senator Vandenberg, in an even less felicitous phrase, advised

5. Walter LaFeber, "American Policymakers, Public Opinion, and the Outbreak of the Cold War, 1945–1950," in Akira Iriye and Yonosuke Nagai (eds.), *The Origins of the Cold War in Asia* (Tokyo, 1977), 52.

Truman that one had to "scare Hell" out of the public to gain support for necessary policy. Beginning in March, 1947, the administration began publicly to equate the need for checking Soviet power with prevention of communist expansion in general.

Synonymous as the Soviet Union and communism were, so too were they identified with benighted forces in conflict with the United States. Opposition to Soviet power was justified to the public as necessary if freedom and liberty were to prevail; in effect, American national interests were associated with enlightened forces struggling for democracy. In an essentially manichean world the stakes were absolute, and the enemy's nefarious designs contrasted sharply with the laudable policies of the United States. The extravagant rhetoric of the anticommunist campaign is best illustrated by the president's speech of March 12, 1947, in which he requested Congress to grant military aid to Greece and Turkey, resisting (respectively) communist-inspired internal subversion and Soviet external pressure. The speech, subsequently famous as the Truman Doctrine, implicitly identified the United States and the Soviet Union with "the ways of life" from which "every nation must choose." One way of life was distinguished by free government, free speech, religious tolerance majority rule, and freedom from oppression; the other was "based upon the will of the minority forcibly imposed upon the majority. It relies upon terror and oppression, a controlled press and radio, fixed elections, and the suppression of personal freedoms." He continued, "I believe it must be the policy of the United States to support free peoples who are resisting attempted subjugation by armed minorities or by outside pressures."[6]

Similar official analyses condemning the adversary's aims while affirming the American belief that, in Woodrow Wilson's words, the United States is "the most unselfish nation in history" were soon forthcoming. Still prevalent isolationist sentiments, Congress's fiscal conservatism, and residual American sympathies for the Soviet Union were thus overcome.

Yet in the ensuing domestic debate, academic and liberal critics—notably Walter Lippmann, Hans J. Morgenthau, and Henry Wallace—argued against policies likely to weaken the United States either by overextending its capabilities or by provoking war with the Soviet Union. Lippmann blasted containment as a "strategic monstrosity," and Reinhold Niebuhr, a staunch supporter of American policy at the time, warned against the willfulness of national pride blind to the dangers of hegemonial purpose.

6. Henry Steele Commager (ed.), *Documents of American History* (2 vols.; New York, 1968), II, 524–26.

Significantly, too, some people in the administration, including the secretary of state, anticipated difficulties related to the president's public explanation of foreign problems. Secretary Marshall feared Truman's speech contained too much flamboyant anticommunism and expressed his doubts to the president about the wisdom of such an overstated presentation. To George Kennan, the administration's successful domestic appeal was tantamount to an absurd call for crusade. He feared that unpredictable public opinion, once alarmed, would drive foreign policy in any direction, likely the wrong one. In 1951, at the height of McCarthyism, Kennan wrote, "People are not always more reasonable than governments . . . public opinion, or what poses for public opinion, is not invariably a moderating force in the jungle of politics."[7] Indeed, the domestic repercussions of a moralistic, ideologically informed policy were troubling. The emotionally provocative portrayal of Washington's policy goals combined with three important features in postwar America—unfulfilled expectations for global harmony, unanticipated international setbacks, and electoral politics—to lead to exaggerated fears of internal subversion and betrayal.

By 1949, members of the Republican party, frustrated over years of Democratic rule, were allied with southern Democrats and exploited popular fears and frustrations. America's foreign problems, such as Berlin and the communist coup in Czechoslovakia, were attributed to an administration "soft on communism" and infiltrated by Soviet spies and sympathizers. A typical attack came from South Carolina's Representative Bryson of the House Committee on Un-American Activities, who proclaimed in 1948 that national security required that "all communists within our borders be rendered politically and economically impotent."[8] The attempts to purge government of subversive agents, of course, exposed few, if any, Soviet spies; however, slander and innuendo were recklessly hurled against a number of public servants and private citizens by sanctimonious politicians, often motivated by personal ambition as much as by concern for the common good.

7. Charles Bohlen, *The Transformation of American Foreign Policy* (New York, 1969), 55; George Kennan, *American Diplomacy, 1900–1950* (Chicago, 1951), 61.
8. Walter Goodman, *The Committee: The Extraordinary Career of the House Committee on Un-American Activities* (London, 1964), 229–30. Pursuing communists and publicity, an investigation of Hollywood actors and writers was undertaken by Congressman John Rankin and colleagues "to expose those elements that are insidiously trying to spread subversive propaganda, poison the minds of your children, distort the history of our country and discredit Christianity." Indeed, Rankin, *de facto* chairman of the Committee on Un-American Activities, was relentless in the struggle against Godless communism, which he claimed "is older than Christianity. It hindered and persecuted the Savior during his earthly ministry, inspired his crucifixion, derided him in his agony, and then gambled for his garments at the foot of the cross."

The administration's domestic policies were unmistakably influenced by the anticommunist campaign. As the 1948 presidential election approached, Truman sought to demonstrate his toughness and deflect opponents' attacks. His 1947 Loyalty Order resulted in the processing of several hundred cases of alleged betrayal and bad security risks in the late 1940s and early 1950s. Many people in the State Department were dismissed, by Truman's own admission years later, "on the flimsiest charges." In 1948 the administration also revived in modern guise the notorious Alien and Sedition Acts and resolved to deport all communist aliens. These and similar episodes add special poignancy to Kennan's plea that in the protracted struggle against Russia "we must have courage and self-confidence to cling to our own methods and conceptions of human society."[9] Although Truman's self-survival methods compromised traditional American values of fairness and due legal process, his maneuvers did not blunt the fury of adversaries anxious to discredit and replace his leadership.

Unlike the administration's successful West European policy—preventing communist expansion and providing the resources and incentives for recovery—the Far Eastern record was eminently vulnerable to criticism. In fact, few American misadventures have caused greater popular debate than the "loss of China." As we have seen, many critics blamed China's subjugation by "international communism" on the White House's general leftist orientation; by "selling out" China, the "Red Dean" and his presidential dupe had jeopardized American security and world peace.

Political pressures and popular doubts aroused by McCarthy forced Secretary Acheson to undertake a "goodwill tour" to convince his compatriots that he was not corrupt, opposed communism, and did not hire traitors. But though the president's support for his secretary prevented the China bloc and McCarthy from taunting Acheson into resigning, less prominent public officials, though equally innocent, were less fortunate. General Hurley's earlier charges against China-based Foreign Service officers Davies, Vincent, Service, and Clubb were revived by McCarthy and his staff; by 1953, only two of more than twenty pre–World War II China-based officers remained in the government's employ. At a time when international events required especially keen sensitivity to Chinese matters, the Division of Far Eastern Affairs was purged of its academic and experience-informed personnel.

The overall effect of McCarthy on the Foreign Service was devastating.

9. Kennan, *Memoirs*, 559.

According to one observer, ''The whole apparatus through which the foreign relations of the United States had to be conducted was in large measure wrecked.'' Even soldier-statesman George Marshall was vilified and implicated in the conspiracy delivering China to the communists. Kennan eventually felt compelled to protest, and in an address to the Century Club (May 7, 1953) he declared:

> I do not see how you can have a satisfactory situation as long as an atmosphere exists in which shibboleths are allowed to be established and to prevail, to the detriment of normal discussion—an atmosphere in which simple alternatives of foreign policy (I am thinking here of such things as the admission of Communist China to the UN) cannot even be discussed without leading to charges of subversion and treason—an atmosphere in which namecalling and insinuation take the place of calm and free debate—an atmosphere in which the dog of government policy gets wagged by the tail of timid, childish, and fantastic internal security arrangements which no one dares to question.

Stalin and other ill-wishers of the United States could only have been secretly pleased with the confusion and damage wrought by McCarthy.

McCarthy's campaign also took a heavy toll on American academic and scholarly writing in public affairs. Previously prominent writers on China featured in newspapers and in journals such as *Harper's*, *Atlantic Monthly*, the *Reporter*, and the *New Republic* were shunned by timorous editors; reliable popular literature on China and Sino-American relations was replaced by turgid, emotional writings purporting to be fair appraisals. The conspiratorial thesis, explaining Far Eastern setbacks, was simple to write and politically safe to expound; unfortunately, the conspiracy and China-as-devil interpretations were not adequately balanced by more dispassionate, analytical works.

Disillusionment and cynicism, then, had arisen by the early 1950s in some important sections of society, creating an atmosphere of increased suspicion. And many critics blurred any sense that gradations of evil existed. Though in practice the State Department and Truman's administration did distinguish the Soviet Union from a more generalized, monolithic communist threat, a great gap had emerged between actual diplomacy and florid official government rhetoric. Aggravating matters was the Truman administration's distrust of the public, which at times bordered on contempt. In May, 1947, Truman reported to the Association of Radio News Analysts, ''Our Government is not a democracy, thank God. It's a republic. We elect men to use their best judgment for the public interest." Acheson later explained, "If you truly had a democracy and did what the people wanted, you'd go wrong every time."[10]

Nevertheless, contrary to the criticism of some contemporary historians, American policy makers in the late 1940s were not involved only with political symbols rather than international realities. True, they had created a myth. True, the myth created domestic problems for the mythmakers and hampered them in achieving their objective with China. Still, they undertook a reasonable policy aimed at dividing the Sino-Soviet alliance. More than the effects of public hounding on the Truman administration, Chinese-American fighting in Korea caused a change in policy from cautious flexibility toward China to intransigence.

The 1952 Republican victory brought to office a group of men acceptable to William Jenner, McCarthy, Bridges, and like-minded others. Secretary of State Dulles, appalled by the rough handling of Dean Acheson, sought to devote himself exclusively to policy issues and distanced himself from the department's administrative problems. This dismal task was assumed by R. W. Scott McLeod, former assistant to Senator Bridges and a dedicated anticommunist. Soon after taking office, McLeod reported, "For the first time in twenty years . . . the House Un-American Activities Committee under Chairman Velde, the Senate Internal Security Subcommittee under McCarthy have received the complete and unequivocal support of the State Department."[11]

Behind his unqualified anticommunist rhetoric, Dulles pursued a policy, as did Truman and Acheson, intended to split or at least greatly impair the Sino-Soviet partnership, and it was partially successful. But meanwhile, an unbridled internal security system—exemplified by the president's Executive Order 10450 of April 27, 1953—inexcusably grew larger and more savage. Hans Morgenthau wrote in 1955, "We are faced with the stark fact . . . that well-meaning and otherwise intelligent men were joined by the great majority of the people in embracing a philosophy of security, which is in truth a mythology, and a policy of security, which is in truth a series of ritualistic performances requiring human sacrifices, both completely divorced from reality and reason."[12]

Could the politics of American diplomacy have been better handled in the late 1940s and 1950s? Instructing and persuading the U.S. public of the vir-

10. LaFeber, "American Policymakers," 60.
11. Ross Koen, *The China Lobby in American Politics* (New York, 1974), 208.
12. Hans Morgenthau, *Politics in the Twentieth Century* (Chicago, 1971), 58.

tues of moderation and the necessity of counterbalancing Soviet power in 1947 assuredly would not have been easy. The likelihood of the public's accepting a policy modestly stated for which the sacrifices were great (such as the costs of maintaining armed forces in Europe and providing generous economic and diplomatic aid to distant lands) and the gains seemingly incremental was at best problematic. Underlying Washington's Cold War rhetoric was the American public's propensity to have its foreign aspirations conform to a moralistic framework peculiarly understood in the United States. For the public to unburden itself of Wilsonian precepts would have been as significant a revolution in American policy thinking as was the decision to "participate" in the postwar world.

Yet, contrary to Acheson, the public mind is not so unsubtle as to be incapable of appreciating, though perhaps not fully comprehending, the complex nature of foreign affairs. If the American public had been dispassionately informed of the magnitude of the Soviet threat, a general consensus likely would have emerged supporting the policy of containment. In any case, American policy should not have been so tied to an ideological-moral root susceptible to vicissitudes in the public mood. This is not to say that the ideological aspect of Soviet-American rivalry could have been ignored, but neither should it have been overly dramatized.

President Truman or Secretary Acheson could have explained simply that Soviet expansion in Europe jeopardized American political and economic interests there and ultimately could imperil American living standards and institutions. Furthermore, a case could have been presented that the United States, though a great power, was unable to rearrange the nature of global politics, that spheres of influence are not inherently insidious, and that playing according to the rules of balance-of-power politics is not *a priori* immoral. It could also have been stated that the United States, while abiding by the United Nations Charter, recognized that the Security Council's structure reflects the less reassuring truths of power and of politics. In other words, policy aims should have been presented for what they were: a set of goals based on calculations of American economic, strategic, and political interests. The United States intended to protect these interests in Europe, Japan, and other areas deemed vital to Washington. But the United States should not have publicly obliged itself to oppose Soviet power wherever it threatened; by so doing American diplomatic maneuverability became needlessly encumbered.

The administration's formulation of America's international problems in 1947 was exaggerated out of any reasonable proportion, hardly proximate to the true situation. Also, a foreign policy presented as indiscriminately anti-communist clouded the fact that the Soviet Union was the real danger and paved the way for later American intervention against national revolutions, themselves invariably cloaked by radical rhetoric and symbols but hardly instruments of Soviet power. Both hostility toward a Marxist-inspired revolutionary movement and official deception of the public by American leaders culminated, years later, in the Vietnam War. By the end of that war, the public had been systematically lied to about America's wartime activities and goals, thereby helping to bring about an unprecedented lack of popular confidence in the country and its institutions.

Clearly, 1947 was a year in which Americans accepted a new direction in one aspect of foreign policy. If they had accepted another—a temperate assessment of international issues—some of the domestic-based problems that dogged the China policy of Truman and Eisenhower could have been avoided. When eventually the United States did come to terms with China, it was Richard Nixon, the anticommunist ideologue of the Cold War, who played a crucial role. He was, ironically, ideally suited for the task of improving relations with the People's Republic. His impeccable anticommunist credentials and record in the 1950s of unqualified hostility to Mao's regime enabled him to overcome most reservations of conservative Americans, who still hailed Taiwan as America's honored client and heroic island of democracy and harbored an abiding revulsion for Chinese communism. Nixon was thus able to elevate Sino-American relations to a realistic plane in which sober calculations of power, balance, and national interest became the publicly accepted primary principles by which to fashion American foreign policy.

To achieve this freedom of diplomatic maneuverability, though, the United States sustained during the Cold War, especially during the late 1940s and early 1950s, considerable and long-term damage to its cultural-political values and foreign policy in general. The diplomatic successes and fleeting wisdom of the early 1970s—themselves now in danger of being superseded by a revived ideological foreign policy—cannot possibly justify the compromising two decades earlier of venerable political traditions and institutions.

BIBLIOGRAPHY

ARCHIVES AND MANUSCRIPT COLLECTIONS

Acheson, Dean. Papers. Truman Library, Independence, Missouri.

Dulles, John Foster. Papers. Princeton University, Princeton, New Jersey.

Dulles-Herter Papers. Eisenhower Library, Abilene, Kansas.

Eisenhower, Dwight D. Papers. Eisenhower Library, Abilene, Kansas.

Elsey, George. Papers. Truman Library, Independence, Missouri.

Francis, Clarence. Papers. Eisenhower Library, Abilene, Kansas.

Jackson, C. D. Papers. Eisenhower Library, Abilene, Kansas.

Kennan, George. Papers. Princeton University, Princeton, New Jersey.

Truman, Harry. Papers. Truman Library, Independence, Missouri.

U.S. Department of State. Records. Record Group 59, National Archives, Washington, D.C.

Lot Files:

Division of Public Affairs.

Office of Chinese Affairs.

Office of Soviet Affairs.

U.S. Department of State and Central Intelligence Agency. Collections. Carrolton Press, Arlington, Virginia.

U.S. Joint Chiefs of Staff. Records. Record Group 218, National Archives, Washington, D.C.

GOVERNMENT PUBLICATIONS

Executive Sessions of the Senate Foreign Relations Committee (Historical Series, Vol. I). 80th Cong., 1st and 2d Sess., 1947–1948. Washington, D.C., 1976.

———. (Historical Series, Vol. II). 81st Cong., 1st and 2d Sess., 1949–1950. Washington, D.C., 1976.

———. (Historical Series, Vol. III, Pt. 1). 82d Cong., 1st and 2d Sess., 1951. Washington, D.C., 1976.

———. (Historical Series, Vol. III, Pt. 2), 82d Cong., 1st and 2d Sess., 1951. Washington, D.C., 1976.

———. (Historical Series, Vol. IV). 82d Cong., 1st and 2d Sess., 1952. Washington, D.C., 1976.

Foreign Relations of the United States, 1946. Vol. IX. Washington, D.C., 1972.

Foreign Relations of the United States, 1947. Vol. VI. Washington, D.C., 1972.

———. Vol. VII. Washington, D.C., 1972.

Foreign Relations of the United States, 1948. Vol. VII. Washington, D.C., 1973.

———. Vol. VIII. Washington, D.C., 1973.

Foreign Relations of the United States, 1949. Vol. VIII. Washington, D.C., 1978.

———. Vol. IX. Washington, D.C., 1974.

Foreign Relations of the United States, 1950. Vol. VI. Washington, D.C., 1976.

Foreign Relations of the United States, 1952–1954. Vol. III. Washington, D.C., 1979.

———. Vol. XVI. Washington, D.C., 1981.

———. Vol. XIII, Pts. 1 and 2. Washington, D.C., 1982.

Senate Committee on Foreign Relations. *The United States and Communist China in 1949 and 1950: The Question of Rapprochement and Recognition.* Staff Study by Robert Blum. Washington, D.C., 1973.

BOOKS

Beloff, Max. *Soviet Policy in the Far East, 1944–1951.* London, 1953.

Blum, Robert. *Drawing the Line: The Origin of the American Containment Policy in East Asia.* New York, 1982.

Bohlen, Charles. *The Transformation of American Foreign Policy.* New York, 1969.

Borg, Dorothy, and Waldo Heinrichs, eds. *Uncertain Years: Chinese-American Relations, 1947–1950.* New York, 1980.

Borisov, O. B., and B. T. Koloskov. *Sino-Soviet Relations, 1945–1973.* Moscow, 1975.

Brandt, Conrad. *Stalin's Failure in China, 1924–1927.* Boston, 1958.

Brodie, Bernard. *War and Politics.* New York, 1973.

Burns, James. *Roosevelt: The Soldier of Freedom, 1940–1945.* London, 1970.

Crankshaw, Edward. *Khrushchev.* Boston, 1970.

Divine, Robert. *Eisenhower and the Cold War Years.* Oxford, 1981.

Djilas, Milovan. *Conversations with Stalin.* New York, 1962.

Dulles, Foster Rhea. *American Policy Toward Communist China, 1949–1969.* New York, 1972.

Floyd, David. *Mao Against Khrushchev*. New York, 1964.

Freeland, Richard. *The Truman Doctrine and the Origins of McCarthyism*. New York, 1974.

Friedman, Edward, and Mark Selden. *America's Asia: Dissenting Essays on Asian-American Relations*. New York, 1971.

Gaddis, John. *Strategies of Containment*. Oxford, 1982.

Gaddis, John, and Thomas Etzold. *Containment: Documents on American Policy and Strategy, 1945–1950*. New York, 1978.

Gittings, John. *Survey of the Sino-Soviet Dispute*. London, 1968.

––––––. *The World and China, 1922–1972*. New York, 1974.

Goodman, Walter. *The Committee: The Extraordinary Career of the House Committee on Un-American Activities*. London, 1964.

Goold-Adams, Richard. *The Time of Power: A Reappraisal of John Foster Dulles*. London, 1962.

Griffith, William. *The Sino-Soviet Rift*. London, 1964.

Hinton, Harold. *The Bear at the Gate*. Stanford, 1971.

––––––. *China's Turbulent Quest*. Bloomington, 1972.

Hoopes, Townsend. *The Devil and John Foster Dulles*. Boston, 1973.

Hudson, G. F.; Richard Lowenthal; and Roderick MacFarquhar. *The Sino-Soviet Dispute*. New York, 1961.

Iriye, Akira, and Yonosuke Nagai, eds. *The Origins of the Cold War in Asia*. Tokyo, 1977.

Kalicki, J. H. *The Pattern of Sino-American Crises*. London, 1975.

Kaplan, Morton. *The Life and Death of the Cold War*. Chicago, 1976.

Kennan, George. *American Diplomacy, 1900–1950*. Chicago, 1951.

Koen, Ross. *The China Lobby in American Politics*. New York, 1974.

LaFeber, Walter. *America, Russia and the Cold War, 1945–1975*. New York, 1976.

Lanyi, George. *Crisis and Continuity in World Politics*. New York, 1973.

Leong, Sow-Theng. *Sino-Soviet Diplomatic Relations, 1917–1926*. Honolulu, 1976.

Low, Alfred. *The Sino-Soviet Dispute*. London, 1976.

MacArthur, Douglas. *A Soldier Speaks*. New York, 1965.

McLane, Charles. *Soviet Policy and the Chinese Communists, 1931–1946*. New York, 1958.

McLellan, David. *Dean Acheson*. New York, 1976.

Mehnert, Klaus. *Peking and Moscow*. New York, 1963.

Morgenthau, Hans. *Politics in the Twentieth Century*. Chicago, 1971.

North, Robert. *Moscow and the Chinese Communists*. Stanford, 1963.

Ponomaryov, B.; A. Gromyko; and V. Khvostov. *History of Soviet Foreign Policy, 1945–1970*. Moscow, 1973.

Purifoy, Lewis. *Harry Truman's China Policy*. New York, 1976.

Randle, Robert. *Geneva 1954*. Princeton, 1969.

Reardon-Anderson, James. *Yenan and the Great Powers*. New York, 1980.

Reitzel, W., Morton Kaplan, *et al. United States Foreign Policy, 1945–1955*. Washington, 1956.

Schram, Stuart. *Mao Tse-Tung*. Middlesex, England, 1975.

———. *The Political Thought of Mao Tse-Tung*. New York, 1969.

Schurmann, Franz. *The Logic of World Power*. New York, 1974.

Simmons, Robert. *The Strained Alliance*. New York, 1975.

Spanier, John. *The Truman-MacArthur Controversy and the Korean War*. New York, 1965.

Stebbins, Richard. *The United States in World Affairs, 1954*. New York, 1956.

Stoessinger, John. *Crusaders and Pragmatists*. New York, 1979.

Sutter, Robert. *China-Watch: Toward Sino-American Reconciliation*. Baltimore, 1978.

Trotsky, Leon. *Leon Trotsky on China*. Edited by Russell Block and Les Evans. New York, 1976.

Tsou, Tang. *America's Failure in China*. Chicago, 1963.

Ulam, Adam. *Expansion and Coexistence*. New York, 1969. 2d ed., 1974.

———. *A History of Soviet Russia*. New York, 1976.

———. *The Rivals*. New York, 1971.

———. *Stalin*. New York, 1973.

Whiting, Allen. *China Crosses the Yalu*. Stanford, 1960.

Zacharias, Ellis. *Behind Closed Doors: The Secret History of the Cold War*. New York, 1950.

Zagoria, Donald. *The Sino-Soviet Conflict*. New York, 1962.

———. *The Sino-Soviet Conflict, 1956–1961*. New York, 1973.

GENERAL REFERENCES

Commager, Henry Steele. *Documents of American History*. Vol. II of 2 vols. New York, 1968.

Daniels, Robert V. *A Documentary History of Communism*. 2 vols. New York, 1960.

The Declassified Documents Reference System. Washington, D.C., 1975–1982.

Grenville, J. A. S. *The Major International Treaties, 1914–1973*. London, 1974.

Nelson, Anna, ed. *The State Department Policy Planning Staff Papers, 1947–1949*. 3 vols. New York, 1983.

The Pentagon Papers. Gravel Edition. 4 vols. Boston, 1971.

Van Slyke, L. P., ed. *The China White Paper*. 2 vols. Stanford, 1967.

MEMOIRS

Acheson, Dean. *Present at the Creation*. New York, 1969.

Adams, Sherman. *Firsthand Report*. New York, 1961.

Eden, Anthony. *Full Circle*. London, 1960.

Eisenhower, Dwight D. *Mandate for Change*. London, 1963.
Kennan, George. *Memoirs, 1925–1950*. Boston, 1967.
Khrushchev, Nikita. *Khrushchev Remembers*. Boston, 1970.
Macmillan, Harold. *Tides of Fortune*. London, 1969.
Rankin, Karl Lott. *China Assignment*. Seattle, 1964.
Sulzberger, C. L. *A Long Row of Candles*. Toronto, 1969.
Trotsky, Leon. *My Life*. New York, 1970.

ARTICLES

Anderson, David. "China Policy and Presidential Politics, 1952." *Presidential Studies Quarterly*, X (Winter, 1980), 79–90.
Bridgham, Philip; Arthur Cohen; and Leonard Jaffe. "Mao's Road and Sino-Soviet Relations: A View from Washington, 1953." *China Quarterly*, LII (October–December, 1972), 670–98.
Gaddis, John. "Was the Truman Doctrine a Real Turning Point?" *Foreign Affairs*, LII (January, 1974), 386–402.
Halperin, Morton, and Tang Tsou. "United States Policy Toward the Offshore Islands." *Public Policy*, XV (1966), 119–38.
Hoffmann, Stanley. "Will the Balance Balance at Home?" *Foreign Policy*, VII (Summer, 1972), 60–86.
Whiting, Allen S. "Communist China and 'Big Brother.'" *Far Eastern Survey*, XXIV (October, 1955), 145–51.

INDEX